EMILY VIKRE

THE
FAMILY
CAMP
COOKBOOK

---- ◆ ----

Easy, Fun, and Delicious Meals to Enjoy Outdoors

HARVARD
COMMON
PRESS

© 2022 Quarto Publishing Group USA Inc.
Text and Photography © 2022 Emily Vikre
Photos © 2022 Hanna Voxland

First Published in 2022 by The Harvard Common Press,
an imprint of The Quarto Group,
100 Cummings Center, Suite 265-D, Beverly, MA 01915, USA.
T (978) 282-9590 F (978) 283-2742 QuartoKnows.com

The Harvard Common Press titles are also available at discount for retail, wholesale, promotional, and bulk purchase. For details, contact the Special Sales Manager by email at specialsales@quarto.com or by mail at The Quarto Group, Attn: Special Sales Manager, 100 Cummings Center, Suite 265-D, Beverly, MA 01915, USA.

26 25 24 23 22   1 2 3 4 5

ISBN: 978-0-7603-7188-6
Digital edition published in 2022
eISBN: 978-0-7603-7189-3

Library of Congress Cataloging-in-Publication Data
Names: Vikre, Emily, author.
Title: The family camp cookbook : easy, fun, and delicious meals to enjoy
    outdoors / Emily Vikre.
Description: Beverly, MA : Harvard Common Press, 2022. |
Includes index. |
    Summary: "From quick snacks to meals you can savor around the campfire,
    The Family Camp Cookbook helps families plan, pack, and cook great food
    in the great outdoors"-- Provided by publisher.
Identifiers: LCCN 2021043115 (print) | LCCN 2021043116 (ebook) | ISBN
    9780760371886 (board) | ISBN 9780760371893 (ebook)
Subjects: LCSH: Outdoor cooking. | Camping--Equipment and supplies. |
    LCGFT: Cookbooks.
Classification: LCC TX823 .V54 2022 (print) | LCC TX823 (ebook) | DDC
    641.5/782--dc23
LC record available at https://lccn.loc.gov/2021043115
LC ebook record available at https://lccn.loc.gov/2021043116

Design and Page Layout: Amy Sly
Photography: Hanna Voxland; except pages 29, 54, 156 are shutterstock

Printed in China

Dedication

For Mom and Dad. Thanks for instilling in me a love of wilderness and of food. I love you to the moon and back.

CONTENTS

Introduction

This is a book about family camping and about cooking, but I'm going to begin it, just briefly, with the Victorians. In college I was fascinated with Victorian cautionary tales. The Victorians were creepily into writing stories that ended poorly for little Jonny and little Elinor as a way of teaching children not to do things such as climb the fence into a pasture with a bull. Now I won't—but I could—write a whole book of camping lessons taught through true-life cautionary tales. For instance, don't strain your pasta over the edge of a cliff lest you lose the pasta—and your pot. Don't forget to bring food that you can eat without cooking, for you may find yourself unable to light a fire or your cook stove in the rain or in the dark. But also don't decide to try to camp for a week with only no-cook food; in particular, don't rely solely on an all-in-one camper's bread recipe from the '70s that turns out to be denser than osmium and harder to chew. Do count how many people are in the car every time you leave a rest station, lest your brother be left behind at a gas station in Nebraska while the family makes it all the way to the next state over before noticing. Name a camping mishap, and someone in our family or friend group has lived it. When I think about family camping, these stories come to mind, and my rational side wrinkles its nose with concern and thinks, "Hang on a minute! Is family camping actually a weird multigenerational hazing ritual?" But, at the exact same moment, my body and heart fill with warm fuzzies and ride a wave of happy associations, golden moments, and deep love. The mishaps weave together with the good times to make a stronger, more complete warp and weft of experience. And isn't that why we take our families camping? To make memories? To spend time together in spite of it all, and even because of it all?

I grew up in a whole community of people who camp as a family, which may be why I have such an abundance of hilarious camping stories. Camping was the main vacation option and summer activity for all the families in our neighborhood. In fact, families often went on their trips *with* other families so that the gaggles of children could amuse one another with sticks and friendship bracelets while the grown-ups chatted. It was just "what you did," and it instilled in all of us kids a sense of wonder in nature and a desire to be outdoors. Clearly the parents of my friends had some sort of superpower, because not only did they take us camping all the time, but they made it look easy. But I'm going to level with you: Camping with kids is *not* particularly easy. However, it is wonderful and worthwhile. You just have to figure out the ropes.

My husband and I used to be quite good at camping. We kept tubs of gear in the basement (actually we still do), lined up and ready to throw in the trunk of a car to get up and go for a weekend trip when the slightest whim hit us. Camping was about spontaneity and freedom. Then we had kids and . . . things changed. At first it seemed like we couldn't camp at all until we realized *you just have to change your expectations and parameters*!

I've found it helps to be aware of and to sort out the different types of fun. Have you heard of the types of fun? Type one fun is just, well, fun. You do things that are fun and you have fun. Type two fun is the fun you have when you push yourself with some kind of challenge. It is difficult and perhaps uncomfortable, but in the end you achieve a goal and the experience psychologically knits itself together to be perceived as fun. As an adult, I've always been pretty into type two fun. I love a good challenge. But my kids . . . my kids are NOT into type two fun. Small people are type one fun people through and through (unless you count jumping off a too-high staircase as type two fun, in which case, my boys are definitely into that). So we rejiggered our outdoor escapades to be more kid friendly. Which, now that I say that, is a completely obvious thing to do. Maybe all other parents realize this stuff right away, but for us it took a while to figure out. Spontaneity was out, planning was in. Hard-core hiking was out, hilarious games of pretending to be baby wild animals that growl, but in a friendly way, while hiking a total of one mile (2 km) were in. And in the end, we all still incidentally wound up with a decent dose of type two fun working its way in there—though the sources are different for me versus my kids.

An absolute ESSENTIAL for maintaining good levels of type one fun is good food. Something to know about me is I'm a food-motivated person. People sometimes say that about their dogs when they're training them: "She's very food-motivated, so she learned to sit and stay real fast once I was holding treats." But the same is true of me as a human. And one of the great joys of camping, whether you're into type two or type one fun, is the food—indeed it's the thing that ties everything together at the end of the day like a bow on a present, regardless of how epic or micro the adventures were.

And even as the type of camping we've done has changed over the years, our camping meals haven't changed much at all.

Eating outside by a campfire is one of the magical aspects of camping that absolutely bonds my family together. A camping trip with good food is a good camping trip, simple as that. And the more comforting the food the better. But, there's no hard and fast rule for what makes a food comforting, or family friendly for that matter. It's deeply personal. I struggled with this a bit as I was choosing the recipes for this book, but in the end I decided to yield to this personal element and focus on sharing the recipes my family loves, giving your family the opportunity to come to love them too. The recipes range from silly simple (mac and cheese, rice cakes with peanut butter) to unexpected (dilly pasta with lamb, cornmeal pancakes with chorizo) to food you mostly prep at home and finish in camp (a big win when you're camping with kids!). For the sake of your sanity, you'll probably want your camping menus to include this range too. Go ahead and lean hard on the tried and true. If, for example, instant oatmeal from a packet and hot dogs grilled over the fire make your camping life happy, then these count as good food! Begin with these basics and sprinkle in a few fun, new recipes here and there. Then again, if you and your family are feeling ambitious, plan to feast! Just remember to bring backup ramen.

I can almost guarantee that when you and your family are licking your sticky s'mores fingers around a crackling campfire, listening to cicadas hum, and marveling at how thickly the stars coat the sky, your kids will be soaking it in, incorporating the joy of the outdoors into the fiber of their beings. Our family friend, Sam Cooke, is an outdoor columnist and last year he wrote up the advice he had given some other friends of ours who were planning to take their six-month-old camping for the first time. His advice was stellar, of course, but his final point, point number twelve, was advice to cherish: "None of this advice matters. You'll do great no matter what and have stories to tell. And someday, looking at the pictures from this trip, your son will figure out how lucky he was to have been born into your family."

And now, without further ado, let's get cooking and camping!

RECOMMENDED COOKING METHOD

Note that the recipes in this book can be cooked one of three different ways: over a fire, on a camp stove, or in a Dutch oven. To make things easy, we've included a symbol next to each recipe that indicates the cooking method we recommend. Adaptable recipes that can be prepped using more than one cooking method include more than one symbol. And, there are some make-ahead recipes that don't involve cooking at camp. Here's a handy-dandy key to those symbols.

 CAMP FIRE   **COOK STOVE**   **DUTCH OVEN**   **MAKE AHEAD**

MEET THE CAMPING EXPERTS

I'm a food professional, but for me camping is a hobby, a fun thing that's unrelated to my career. And truth be told, I get a niggling uncomfortable feeling when I write about things that I don't have multiple degrees in. I looooooove expertise (it drives my husband crazy). So, while working on this book I decided to loop in some experts who could give some additional tips. Luckily, I didn't have to go far. One of my childhood friends, Kaitlin, was part of the enthusiastic camping village I grew up in. Her parents, Mark and Sherry, were (and still are) flat-out camping geniuses, and Kaitlin went on to become a professional canoe guide who also runs an outdoor children's school. She has three kids of her own and is married to an outdoor guide. So it was natural to ask her—and her parents!— to get involved with this book. Not only did her expertise guide some of my choices and recommendations, you'll see some sidebars from her sprinkled throughout. Let's meet Kaitlin, one of my lifelong besties!

Kaitlin: "I grew up in a camping kind of family. Backwoods canoe camping, car camping, pop-up trailer camping, we did it all. My parents were canoe guides in the Boundary Waters Canoe Area Wilderness of northern Minnesota when they were in college, and they loved to take the three of us kids to the woods whenever they had a free moment. I have grand childhood memories of sunrise paddles, fires sparking up to the stars, magical encounters with wildlife, and falling asleep to the wind in the pines. I also have less grand memories of dashing from the tent to the car for protection from severe weather, and of my dad grabbing my one-year-old sister's hair to keep her from falling into the campfire.

While as a twenty-one-year-old canoe guide I could paddle and portage all day, sleep on the ground, eat anything put in front of me, and cheer on my middle-school-aged campers, things have changed. As an almost forty-year-old mother of three children under three-and-a-half years old, I have had to completely relearn how to camp. Luckily, my husband and I are a good team and we're on the same page—it's all about survival when you're camping with young children. (Note though that every family will have their own favorite tips and tricks. Ask around and learn from everyone you meet on your adventures!)

Probably the biggest lesson I've learned is to slow down and tone down my expectations. Now our adventures are kid-sized adventures, or micro-adventures, as we call them. We may paddle a kayak from a nearby beach out to Duluth's iconic Aerial Bridge or bike under the stately pines in the neighborhood park. It's not the twenty-six-mile (42 km) day of paddling from dawn to dusk that we used to do back when we were young. The beautiful and important part of our current adventures is that we're out as a family moving our bodies, getting fresh air, and helping the children develop connections with the natural world. It's the same with camping. The goal is to go for it, to build memories, to get the children hooked on outdoor adventures when they are young so they'll want to go outside their whole lives. I think it's working because I heard my son Seppo say recently, "We should go camping soon. It's so peaceful. Maybe we'll hear an owl!"

CHAPTER ONE

The
CAMPING
KITCHEN

When it comes to eating successfully on the trail, a little planning goes a long way. Actually, unless you are trained as a survivalist, it ALL comes down to planning. And the more people of different ages you have with you, the more planning and preparation you will want to do. For many people I know, this is a huge part of the fun of camping, the checklists and the weeks spent thinking through menus and creating shopping lists and charts of packing responsibilities. That's really not me. Lists and planning make me chafe and fill me with a mounting sense of anxiety, but here they are for you anyway because that's how important they are! So buckle up, read this whole chapter, and use it as a checklist if you wish.

Let's Gear Up!

I am the type of camper who says, "Let's keep using the same camping equipment we have had for the past thirty years because it has worked so far and it only has a few holes in it." In other words, I don't have recommendations for the crème de la crème of the newest camping gadgets. But our approach does mean our family has a pretty dialed-in list of our camp cooking must-haves.

COOLER

Throughout this book I'm assuming you're car camping, and a cooler—or two—is at the center of your food storage. A good cooler with adequate ice allows you to have all sorts of fresh ingredients, making it possible to eat like a gourmand in the woods. There is a variety of coolers on the market now with super thick insulated walls that will keep food plenty chilled for three to four days at a time, if not longer. If possible, bring two coolers, one for food and one for drinks. This will allow you to keep your food colder longer as you won't need to open either cooler for as many things. For a complete set of cooler packing tips, check the "Stay Chill" section (page 21).

CAMP COOK STOVE

You could try to cook over the fire only, but that's basically inviting rain and logs that won't catch fire, or conversely a fire ban, and general disaster. Bring a cook stove so you can at least make your kids' favorites in a pinch, which for me means macaroni and cheese. With a good camp stove, you can cook pretty much just as you would on a stovetop at home, with slightly less precise temperature control. Most camp stoves these days even have a self-igniter and built-in nozzle cleaners, and don't cause nearly the problems or cautionary tales of woe from camp stoves of yore.

If you're car camping, more is better, and I recommend turning to a trusty two-burner propane stove. My friend Kaitlin has her own set of opinions though, so check out her favorites in the "Tips from a Wilderness Guide: Choosing Cooking Methods" box on page 20.

Whichever camp stove option you are using, make sure you bring enough fuel. If most of your cooking is happening over the fire, you can get away with one to two canisters for a weekend. But if you're planning on lots of cooking and feasting for a large crew of campers, you might want to have one canister for every one to two meals!

TYPES OF CAMP STOVES
An Overview

Though I'm a two-burner stalwart, there is a variety of different camp stove genres available, and something different may suit your family best. Here are the general categories of stoves to consider.

TABLETOP TWO-BURNER STOVES

The Coleman two-burner is the old faithful of camping stoves. There is a variety of brands these days, but as a general rule these stoves use propane canisters and the lid folds up into a wind screen. These have fairly powerful and somewhat adjustable burners, and they work in inclement weather. Take a look at some of the options online and buy one that fits your budget. If you want the specific Coleman your parents had with the white gas tank that you pressurize with a little plunger, these days it's called the "Guide Series Dual-Fuel." In my opinion, a tabletop two-burner is *the* way to go if you're car camping.

SINGLE-BURNER REFILLABLE STOVES

We've done a lot of camp cooking over an old MSR WhisperLite, one of many lightweight folding stoves that use white gas or alcohol. If you want getting your stove started to be a big part of the trip, one of these stoves may be for you! But there are also some quite ingenious systems in this category, including the Swedish Trangia system, which uses a simple alcohol burner with a nesting system of aluminum pots. There are also some very nifty DIY alcohol stoves you can make from tuna cans! If you're going to be carrying your stove and fuel, it may be worth making some sacrifices for lightness, but keep in mind that some of those sacrifices may include stability, adjustability, and reliability. In general, these single-burner stoves are not for the average family camping trip.

If you need to use one, definitely make sure you familiarize yourself with your stove's operation before it's make or break to get food on the table.

SINGLE-BURNER CARTRIDGE STOVES

There are many types of one-burner cartridge stoves available that use disposable butane or propane cartridges, some with a built-in cooking pot system, such as the Jet Boil. These stoves are very easy to use, fast, and fairly adjustable. Most of them screw right onto the canister though, meaning the cooking surface is up high, and a precarious pot of boiling water isn't the best thing when there are kids around. So like the single-burner refillable, there's probably a better option for most family trips.

BIOMASS STOVES

There are a few stoves out there that are a sort of enhanced version of cooking over a wood fire, using twigs and careful air management. The Bushbuddy and Solo Stove are two good options. If you want to be high tech about your low-tech cooking, the BioLite stove was invented by some of my husband's college classmates and will allow you to charge your phone while you cook dinner.

TWO SKILLETS

I recommend having two different sizes of skillets if you can swing it, one 10-inch (25 cm) and one 12-inch (30 cm). A 12-inch (30 cm) cast-iron skillet may be heavy, but it makes up for it by being able to cook darn near anything all while toning your biceps in the process. Cast iron is nice because you can use it on a camp stove, or over a campfire on a grate, or even sitting directly in coals. And they last forever. In fact, the best cast iron is vintage cast iron. Just make sure you never use soap to clean it. Scrape it out and rub it down, and it's ready to go again. We also use aluminum skillets with detachable handles for a lot of adventures because they are lightweight and good for plenty of frying or sautéing applications, ranging from pancakes to vegetables.

TWO POTS

It's helpful to have one large pot for heating soup or boiling noodles, and a smaller pot for things such as rice, couscous, oatmeal, hot cocoa, and desserts.

CAMPING DUTCH OVEN

Not a necessity per se, but if you're car camping and you can lug plenty of stuff with you, it can be really fun to have a Dutch oven so that you can bake a cake or rolls. There's nothing that says, "I'm good at this," like whipping up a Dutch oven cake after dinner. And, you might find that using a camping Dutch oven is way easier than you think. But more on that in the "Dutch Oven Primer" section (page 25).

The classic camping Dutch ovens are made of cast iron and have little legs and a rimmed lid that so you can pile hot coals on top of it. Personally, I have an anodized aluminum Dutch oven, and I absolutely love it. It's lightweight, and it's capable of pretty much anything I've asked of it in the baking-with-fire department. Dutch ovens are usually 10-inch (25 cm) or 12-inch (30 cm), and they can be shallow or deep. I like a deep one because then you can bake with it or use it for soups and chili. And I find most of the time the 10-inch (25 cm) size is suitable for our family of four because (a) our kids are still fairly young and don't eat that much, and (b) I'm usually baking with it, and 10 inches (25 cm) is the best size for baking.

CAMPING KNIVES

You'll want a pocketknife for applications such as marshmallow stick carving and pulling out the tiny scissors to make amusing paper animals as a source of distraction when dinner is still cooking and your kids are wondering why they can't watch shows. But, you'll also want at least one (if not two) larger knives for chopping ingredients and slicing cheese, and you'll definitely want the knife to have a sheath to prevent dangerous accidents and to make packing it easy. You can buy knives that come with sheaths, but you can also make a decent sheath out of thick cardboard and duct tape.

CUTTING BOARD

We generally bring just one lightweight cutting board and use plates as cutting boards if more are needed.

UTENSILS GALORE

You'll need utensils to cook and eat with. You can buy specialized camping utensils, but I think that's totally unnecessary. Just hit up a garage sale or estate sale and procure a set of all the utensils on this list, designate them as your camping utensils, and voilà, that's what they are! Here's my list of essentials:

- Knives, forks, and spoons

- Unbreakable plates and bowls of any sort. We usually use old-school aluminum camping plates, but they are kind of tricky because they get hot and can burn little hands, so enamelware, plastic plates, or melamine are also good options. (Enamelware and melamine have the added benefit of looking cute.)

- Camp cups! For all your imbibing needs. Most importantly, you'll need mugs for coffee. Coffee mugs also work fine for water, lemonade, wine, and cocktails, but you might also want to bring a few other cups that aren't coffee cups, plus a designated cup in a different favorite color for each kid in the group to avoid squabbles.

- Wooden stirring spoon for literally anything. With a good wooden spoon, you will find yourself well-near invincible in the cooking department.

- Spatula for flipping things such as pancakes

- Ladle (in a pinch, a big spoon can also work for things such as serving soup)

- Very long tongs for all fire-related cooking

- Can opener

- Grater. Instead of a box grater, we have one that is a little flat rectangular grater on a handle. It is pretty fantastic for grating things such as carrots or cheese.

- Wine bottle opener and/or bottle opener (unless everything you bring is in cans or transferred to other containers, which totally works)

- Aluminum foil

- Heat-resistant gloves (I like my husband's welding gloves when I'm cooking with fire) or oven mitts

Camping Considerations

WATER STORAGE AND WATER TREATMENT OPTIONS. Your camping trip won't last long if you don't have good water. You'll need it for drinking, cooking, and cleaning. Before you leave, make sure you know exactly what kinds of water options you'll have available wherever you'll be camping and plan accordingly. If you are bringing water, it's a good idea to bring twice as much as you think you'll need. Jerry cans, large water bladders, and water coolers are all good options for water storage. And they're useful even if you are at a campground with potable water because it means you won't have to be making a million trips to the water pump. If you are treating your own water, my personal favorite method is using a system with a hand pump through a purifier, but you can also use methods such as UV wands, boiling, or even good old-fashioned iodine tablets, though I've never met a kid who didn't despise the taste of iodine.

INGREDIENT STORAGE. I find camp cooking with kids around is about a million times easier if I get as much prep work done at home as possible. Vegetables can be transported prechopped, spices can be transported premixed, and so on. A good set of leak-proof stackable containers is life changing in this regard. It allows you to transport prepped meal ingredients and then store leftovers in the emptied containers so that you don't waste anything. Your containers don't need to be camping specific, just sturdy and tight sealing. But, in the camping department, Nalgene makes a variety of small containers that are fantastic for holding spices and spice blends or for storing small amounts of liquids if you have any special oils or vinegars but don't need the whole bottle. Also, though I am deeeeeeeeply opposed to gadgets that have only one use, I will concede that a special rigid egg case is an extremely worthwhile thing to have!

COFFEE-MAKING SETUP. Coffee is a major food group for my husband and me, so a good coffee setup is an absolute must. We cannot survive without it nor would we want to. There's more about coffee in the breakfast chapter, so for now I'll just say choose your coffee setup, make sure you have ALL the pieces you need for it (quadruple check), and bring at least three times more coffee than you anticipate needing. If your kids are young, like ours, they probably won't go to sleep until it is far past bedtime, they'll wake up throughout the night to ask where they are, they'll get up at the crack of dawn while owls are still hooting, and you'll be able to put on a cheerful face through all of it because you have enough coffee.

DISHWASHING SETUP. It's not the most fun part of cooking in camp, but cleaning everything up when you are done cooking and eating is oh so important for keeping the experience pleasant. And, in fact, kitchen patrol duty is an EXCELLENT assignment for older children. They'll feel so helpful! They'll make memories! Make sure you have a basin or large pot for hot water (get your water heating off to one side of the fire while you're cooking the main meal), biodegradable soap, and a scrub brush. Some people like to bring a scraper for scraping pots and dishes, but I've never owned one, and I've managed to make it this far using a spatula for scraping. If you do need a scraping assist, an old credit card works wonders and takes up zero extra space. It also works for scraping frost off your windshield if you need to! If you have space, it can be nice to bring a little collapsible dish-drying rack, but we generally just bring a few dishtowels (we use them for wrapping things during the transporting-to-camp process) and get things wiped dry right away. If your campsite doesn't have a specific place for dumping dish water, make sure to teach the child—or adult—on cleanup duty how to toss the dish water away from where you are camping and at least 200 feet (61 m) from any water source, dispersing it in a wide spray so it evaporates easily.

FIRE-STARTING SETUP. If you are camping at a site that allows fire, make sure the wood you are using is from nearby or purchased on site so that you do not accidentally introduce invasive insects to the area. No one wants that on their conscience. Many campsites have a place where you can buy firewood. However, this firewood is usually in large logs, so you'll want to bring a small wood-splitting hatchet because unless you are a wizard with a staff that shoots firebolts or you are Kaitlin's husband Matti (which is kind of the same thing), it is not possible to start a fire with big logs. You need small logs first. And good kindling. Make sure you also have a good way to start a fire, whether it's matches, a lighter, or my preferred method, a blow torch (aka "boy scout matches"). It's also not a bad idea to bring one or seven of those paraffin and wood chip fire starters. I have had great luck with those.

OTHER. Again, sometimes more is better, and if you're going for a posh wilderness experience with minimal whining, it often is. It can be nice to bring a variety of other elements for creature comforts. Here are a few things we always bring:

- Tarp with ropes to hang over the picnic table in case of drizzle

- Oilcloth tablecloth for covering the picnic table. This is a trick I learned from Kaitlin, who needs to make sure she can protect herself from any potential gluten left over from earlier campers. But it's also nice for easy cleanup and for cute-ing up the campsite.

- Extra folding table for more surface area for cooking, eating, and setting up favorite games for the kids

- Comfortable camp chairs for relaxing by the fire

- Large tubs for keeping all your gear organized. It is helpful to have a sizable assortment of tubs so you can use them to store your gear at home so it's ready and waiting for you when you and your family decide you want to get out of town for a weekend. In fact, this may be the difference between going and not going. (Trust me, I've been there.)

Tips from a Wilderness Guide
CHOOSING COOKING METHODS

WITH KAITLIN

The options are endless when it comes to methods for cooking while camping. You can use everything from a specialized stove that will boil water in 60 seconds flat, to cooking over the fire, to using a one- or two-burner camp stove. My family prefers cooking over a fire whenever possible because it's part of the ambiance and ritual of camping for us. It smells amazing, it's quiet, it's charming, and there's plenty of space for multiple pots and dishes. There's also an art to building and cooking over a fire that brings us right back to our canoe guiding days. However, it does take a good deal of time and a wee bit of skill to build and maintain a fire suitable for cooking and cook a full meal over it. We always bring a backup in case we want to have a quicker meal, can't procure the correct amount of firewood, or need to cook over the stove on the side. Our preferred stove is a Swedish Trangia because it is completely silent and very compact for packing.

You may find it most convenient to plan to cook over the fire for dinners and for breakfasts on lay-over days (days when you don't travel to a new campsite) since fire cooking takes longer. You can then use your stove for cooking on a morning when you want to get out of camp more quickly. Likewise, you can plan a quicker breakfast, such as granola or oatmeal, for a travel day instead of a breakfast such as pancakes that may take you half the morning to pull off.

We've also started bringing a Bushbuddy twig stove when we're car camping so that we can cook coffee, or boil water for the kids' hot cocoa, while oatmeal is going on the Trangia. You still get a bit of the feeling of a breakfast fire but on a smaller and more efficient scale. Kids are drawn to the tiny Bushbuddy stove. It's adorable. And, the stove uses twigs for fuel, so kids of many ages can be very involved in grabbing twigs from all over the campsite and feeding them into the fire.

I recommend having a premade dinner that can be eaten cold or simply reheated for your first night. When you arrive at your destination, the kids will be very busy exploring the new place, and there is lots of work to do to prepare your campsite if you are tent camping. It's also possible that you are running late and arrive after the check-in time, which means that you may not be able to buy firewood for heating your meal. In many locations, it's illegal to transport firewood across county lines due to invasive species.

Stay Chill
TIPS FOR PACKING YOUR COOLER

How you pack your cooler is as important as what kind of cooler you use. Luckily, there are some universally applicable cooler-packing tips that will make you look like the king or queen of chill.

1. Get that cooler clean! Hopefully, you wiped your cooler down well after the last time you used it. My friend Jessica once left a bunch of chicken carcasses in a cooler in the garage and only discovered them after her mom got out the cooler a year later because they were going on a family road trip.) Then wash it down again before you pack it. It's always a good idea to disinfect it as well. Plain white vinegar works great for this.

2. If you can, chill your cooler in advance. The colder your cooler is inside before you pack it, the longer it will stay cool. To prechill your cooler, fill it with ice water for about twelve hours before use, then drain and pack it.

3. Make sure all your food is cold as well. Prep as much food as you can and transfer it to sealed containers to chill before you go. Freeze as many foods as you can, including meats and soups, and pack these frozen. Oh, and make sure all your food is in waterproof packaging. No matter how well you chill everything, your ice will melt over time, and there are few things ickier than soggy turkey or hot dog–infused melt water.

4. Plan your packing. Map out your meals and load them into the cooler in reverse order, so the food for your last day is on the bottom, second to last day is above that, and so on. Keep dinner foods on one side and breakfast and lunch foods on the other.

5. Lay down reusable ice packs as your very bottom layer. Then pack your food, filling in all the cracks between with ice. Leave as little space for air as possible.

6. Make a separate cooler for drinks. Icy cold margaritas for you and fruit-infused ice water for the kids? Luxury! And if your drinks have their own little cooler, they won't have to compete with the kebabs for space.

7. In camp, keep your cooler in a shady place and open it as little as possible. The cooler you keep it and the less warm air you let in, the longer it will hold its chill and the better it will keep your food.

8. Don't drain the ice melt water. I know. I hate, hate, hate leaving ice melt water in my cooler. However, science has shown that leaving the melt water in there keeps everything colder, and I respect science. But, consider this yet another reminder to make sure all your food is in leak-proof, watertight packaging.

Let's Cook with Fire!

Campfires and campfire cooking are one of the profound pleasures of camping, if not one of the main reasons for going camping at all! You can proudly think to yourself, "I am human. I control fire." Just make sure you really are controlling your fire. First you need to know how to build it.

HOW TO START A FIRE (WHEN YOU SUCK AT STARTING A FIRE)

Ironically, neither my husband nor I are particularly good at starting fires. It's even funnier in the case of my husband, who spent a year living in rural Kenya where all of his cooking was done over the fire. But he was so bad at starting fires, the village children would always intervene and do it for him. This was nice of them, but he never improved! Similarly, an abnormally large proportion of my friends are professional outdoor guides, so I am rarely the person who has fire starting on their agenda. I'm the cook but not the fire builder.

That said, I can be perfectly fine at starting fires when I get the conditions right, so I focus on creating the ideal setup. Start with good tinder. Lots of paper, birch bark, or a fire starter is an absolute must. Do not try to start a fire without something that will catch fire easily. Next, make sure you have plenty of small twigs that will also catch fire easily. Be sure you have small branches or dry, split logs to add once your twigs are burning happily. If you rush to large logs, you'll smother your fire. So, kindling first, then twigs, then small branches, then small firewood, then finally add some small-medium logs. When the small-medium logs are burning well, that's when I recommend adding a large log or two.

I am a firm believer in the method of fire building where you start by adding your firewood in a teepee shape, but once things are hot and chugging along in flaming fashion, you can chuck in more logs as needed.

I am also a firm believer in having a powerful fire starting back up. If you can't start your fire with matches and all your kindling, I have to admit it's pretty satisfying to hold a blowtorch up to a log until it succumbs, and you have fire.

Most campsites have a fire pit or fire ring, and that is definitely where you should build your fire. Don't go rogue. It's not worth the fire hazard. If for some reason you find yourself in a situation where you need to create your own fire pit, first make sure you are minimum of 30 feet (9 m) away from anything flammable, dig a pit in the dirt, then make a ring of large rocks around it to create a fireproof barrier. But, truly, under such circumstances might I suggest you ask yourself what in the world you are doing, and then stick with your camp stove.

NOW WE'RE COOKING!

Cooking food over fire is all about managing your heat and trusting your instincts about what is too hot, what is not hot enough, and when your food is adequately cooked. Cook times and specific instructions go out the window when it comes to fire, so you have to pay attention to sensory cues such as how your food looks and smells and make your decisions based on that.

Many campsites have a grate over the fire pit, which you can use for putting pots on or use like a grill. But you may also want to provide your own grate so that you will be assured that you have one, and it will typically have grill bars that are closer together. You can buy a handy camping grate on foldable legs and tote it with you wherever your adventures take you.

You don't want to cook food over a high flame. Let your fire burn down to hot coals, and make sure you have accounted for the time this takes when you are planning your cooking start time. When you are ready to cook, you want to do what is called grading your coals in order to create different zones of heat. Using your long tongs or the best fire tool of them all—a long stick—spread your coals so that you have a thick, hotter layer of coals for medium-high cooking on one side of your fire pit and a sparser layer of coals on the other side for lower-heat cooking. Pay attention to your food as it cooks. Does it seem like it's going too fast? Then spread your coals out more. Too slow? Pile the coals higher and maybe add another little piece of wood off to the edge to start to burn into more coals. It's not optimal practice, but I've never been one to fixate on optimal practice, so I will say sometimes (okay, often) I also have the fire going actively on one side of the pit while I rake coals over to the other side, and then I cook over on the coal side while letting the fire side crackle happily for ambiance. Alternatively, I let the fire burn down to coals, do my cooking, then build the fire back up for ambiance when the food is done.

Dutch Oven Primer

For years, I found the idea of Dutch oven cooking paralyzingly intimidating. I would read up on how to do it, including all the instructions about briquettes and doing math to determine briquette numbers and coal ratios and I thought, "That is soooo not my style. I don't even measure things or time them most of the time; I'm not suddenly going to start doing briquette math. No thanks." That is until the day Kaitlin's parents taught me to make corn bread in a Dutch oven. They just put their Dutch oven on the grate over the fire, and then they actually started a small twig fire on the lid. They casually fed the twig fire until they felt like maybe the bread was done. When they lifted the lid and checked, lo and behold, there was a fluffy and delicious corn bread, with no math or otherwise intimidating steps taken.

From that moment on, I decided Dutch oven cooking was totally my style, because when it comes down to it, all you need to do is keep your pot hot until it's baked. You can also say that sentence out loud and get a laugh from all the adults in your group. So, here's what I do: I let the fire burn down to hot coals. I either place the Dutch oven and its contents on a grate over the coals, or I use tongs to build a ring of coal pieces on a heat-resistant surface (I use an old metal garbage can lid that we bring with us). I put the covered Dutch oven onto the ring of coals, then I pile a bunch more coals from the fire on top. No counting, no nothing. Then I wait. Every now and then I add more coals if it feels like the ones on the oven lid are getting too cool. Also, every now and then I lift the lid of the Dutch oven with my tongs (you can get specialized lid lifters, but I don't use one) to check the progress of my baked good. This also lets out a bit of steam. If it's not done yet, I return the lid and keep waiting. If it is done, I use the Dutch oven handle and my long tongs to lift the oven off the coals or grate and set it somewhere to cool. I use the tongs to remove the lid and dump the coals back into the fire as well. Don't forget to wear your heat-resistant gloves whenever you are cooking with a Dutch oven over coals.

If you are not like me and you do love precision, here is some recommended Dutch oven math: Multiply the diameter of the oven by two. This is the number of briquettes (or briquette-sized wood coals) you should use. Place one-third of them below the Dutch oven and two-thirds above to create an oven that is about 375°F (190°C).

Tips from a Wilderness Guide
KAITLIN'S TIPS FOR NAVIGATING KIDS AND FIRE

Fire is mesmerizing. Adults and children alike love to stare into the embers of a burning fire. If you are using fire for cooking, even if it's just to make s'mores, the children in your crew will be drawn to the fire and will want to help.

Here are some tips for using fire with children:

- Teach your child fire safety.

- Children should always be supervised near fires.

- Fire is not a toy.

- Teach and model how to pay attention to where your body is in relation to the hot grate, cooking pots, and fire.

- Teach your child to use appropriate safety equipment, such as heavy-duty fire gloves to protect their hands while feeding the fire or stirring a pot of food.

- Teach your child to have a water bucket nearby in case an ember lands on the ground and starts smoldering or smoking.

- Teach them to use a lighter and matches safely and how to dispose of used matches.

- Practice good stewardship. Talk with your child about firewood restrictions that are in place in your location and practice following them as a family. Typical restrictions might include not transporting firewood from outside of the county, gathering only dead, downed wood that is away from the campsite, not cutting standing trees for firewood, and not pulling birch bark from live trees.

- Teach your child fire-building techniques such as placing twigs to form a teepee shape with birch bark or other fire starter in the middle.

- Let the child participate with the fire in a way that fits with their age and stage. Younger children can help gather firewood and help you add the twigs to the fire in the grate or on top of the Dutch oven; older youth will be very engaged in trying to light a fire on their own.

- Letting an older child be in charge of making and tending the fire on top of a Dutch oven is a great way to let them learn about and experiment with fire in a controlled way.

Planning Your Menus and Hitting the Road

When you plan out your camping trip menu, think about what your family likes to eat and how much time you really want to spend cooking. There is no right or wrong answer: Just think about what works for you. On some trips, the best part may be cooking elaborate meals while you enjoy hanging out by the fire. On others, meals need to be fast and convenient because you're going to be mostly on the go. Or you might choose a mix where a portion of the meals are more cooking intensive while others are prepped at home and just need to be heated (or not even heated) and served. Plan your menus so that you use up the most perishable foods on the first couple of days of camping while later meals rely more on dried or canned ingredients. Also, there is nothing wrong with eating the same thing for breakfast and lunch every day. Finally, make sure you have a variety of bail-out meals such as boxed macaroni and cheese, dried soup for rehydrating, plenty of pitas and peanut butter, and plenty of chocolate. There are few situations that cannot be saved with a hefty dose of chocolate.

SAMPLE THREE-DAY MENUS

Kinda Classic Menu

DAY ONE
Arrival dinner: hot dogs, Norwegian stick bread, grilled corn
Arrival dessert: s'mores—duh

DAY TWO
Breakfast: skillet biscuits with jam, scrambled eggs, coffee
Lunch: classic camping sandwich, apples, trail mix
Dinner: one-pot beef stroganoff, new old-fashioneds to drink
Dessert: caramelized apple skillet crisp

DAY THREE
Breakfast: the best fluffy pancakes, coffee
Lunch: curried tuna salad with rye crisps; clementine oranges; lemonade, beer, or canned cocktails
Dinner: foil-baked sweet potatoes with toppings
Dessert: grilled fruit or banana boats

Pretty Gourmet Menu

DAY ONE
Arrival dinner: pita pizzas, pineapple basil gimlets
Arrival dessert: campfire cobbler

DAY TWO
Breakfast: Dutch oven sweet rolls, fried eggs, fruit
Lunch: turkey and guacamole wraps, apricot-pistachio bites
Dinner: kebab fajitas
Dessert: cracker crust pudding pie

DAY THREE
Breakfast: eggs in purgatory
Lunch: chickpea salad and pitas, homemade granola bars
Dinner: Widgi's meat and cheese board with wine, followed by decorate your own ramen bowls
Dessert: tea, chocolate

Hearty Vegetarian Menu

DAY ONE
Arrival dinner: creamy tomato soup with grilled cheese
Arrival dessert: Dutch oven strawberry cake

DAY TWO
Breakfast: Norwegian pancakes with strawberry jam
Lunch: farmer's lunch sandwich
Dinner: Milena's dried wild mushroom risotto
Dessert: mulled wine, hot chocolate, grilled fruit

DAY THREE
Breakfast: strawberries and cream oatmeal
Lunch: rye crisps with hard-boiled egg
Dinner: chickpea and couscous bowls, summer fruit cups to drink
Dessert: banana boats

Tips from a Wilderness Guide
KEEPING YOUR FOOD SAFE WHILE CAMPING

Be sure to research the requirements for protecting your food at each destination. It's not good for wildlife or people if critters of any size get used to finding their food in campsites. If you are van, car, or camper camping, you will likely need to store your food in a hard-sided vehicle or in a bear box any time you are not in your campsite. It's easy enough to keep a cooler inside your vehicle. We generally pack our dry food items in a large plastic storage bin with a tight-fitting lid to keep everything in one spot and keep small critters such as squirrels, chipmunks, and mice out of our food. We pick a large enough size to store the utensil roll, plastic kid dishes, and other small camping cookware in the bin to efficiently pack and keep critters from climbing in or chewing on the dishes and silverware overnight (yuck!).

Backcountry campsites may have a bear box, or you may need to carry a bear barrel, which is a bear-proof, lightweight plastic barrel that comes in many sizes, and you either fit it in a pack or wear the barrel itself as a pack. Some areas may require you to hang a bear pack, which means hanging your food pack high in a tree so that bears can't reach it from the ground or from a nearby tree. If you're not familiar with hanging a bear pack, definitely look up how to do it before your trip. At the least, you'll need a long, sturdy rope or two and a plan for how to throw one end of the rope high enough in a tree. There are methods of hanging a bear pack with pulleys

that I definitely recommend. The ultimate bear pack setup is when you can throw a rope over a high branch on one tree and then the same rope over a high branch on a tree across a clearing. Then, you hang the bear pack over that rope using a second rope and a pulley. Very slick. A perfect bear pack is something to brag about when you get home after your trip.

Throwing a bear rope can provide a whole afternoon of entertainment. I've seen people go to extraordinary, humorous, and even slightly dangerous lengths to get the rope over just the right branch. You need to have enough weight to get the rope up into the tree and over the branch. Just please don't tie your rope around a rock to get it over the branch you have in mind. The rock is likely to come crashing down upon your head or come flying out of the rope at just the right angle to nail a fellow camper. You probably don't want to tie your water bottle to the rope either; I've seen poor water bottles abandoned in trees after getting stuck. Our preferred method is to wind (not knot) the rope around itself to create a baseball-sized clump of rope just heavy enough to toss. As you throw the rope, it will, in theory at least, unravel over the branch and fall perfectly at your feet so you can tie on the pack.

DON'T LEAVE WITHOUT A CAMPING-READY MINDSET

Camping with kids is different from camping by yourself or with other adults. It's harder, if I'm honest. Depending on the age of the kids, it may be a LOT harder; or they may be at the sweet age where they are old enough to be engaged and to sleep at the appropriate time but not so old that they are surly and back to sleeping at all the inappropriate times. No matter what, bringing young people into the wilderness can instill in them a lifelong sense of wonder and love for nature that makes it all worth the effort. Plus, we all need to be wrenched away from our reliance on screens, and camping is one of the few ways that seems to be really effective. All this said, with the right attitude, even a tough camping trip without much sleep spent chasing busy young ones can still be a joy. Here are some tips we have rounded up from our community of campers:

- Don't plan a camping trip during the buggy season. It's not worth it. Even a moose can't survive under those conditions. But definitely do plan a camping trip when the sun has started to set a little earlier again, as this will increase your chances of getting some sleep.

- Bring lots of comfort items and a few favorite toys, games, and bedtime stories. Never underestimate the power of a favorite book or Lego set.

- Plan a short trip. Family camping trips do not need to be displays of athletic prowess or tough-it-out games of chicken, unless your kids are teenage boys of the ilk my brothers were, in which case that may be just what the doctor ordered.

- Invest in a really big tent and nice camping mattresses. Why not? I mean yes, it is true that a big tent and inflatable mattresses are so fun that it might cause the kids to bounce off the walls and never want to do anything other than play in the tent. This is the reason for mandatory hikes. Mandatory hikes at least come with mandatory chocolate.

- Go with another family so that adults can trade off child supervising and cooking duties. Plus, camping with another family is a sure way to forge a lifelong, unbreakable bond of friendship. And if you're lucky, at least one member of the group plays guitar so you can have embarrassing campfire sing-alongs.

- Bail if you need to. There is a Norwegian mountain rule that says, *Vend i tide, det er ingen skam å snu*, which translates to "Turn around before it's too late. There is no shame in going back." It's about watching for mountain storms, but I say the same goes for camping. If you need to cut your trip short because of weather or another reason, it's fine. You can try again next time.

Okay, are you ready? I'm ready! Let's go camping!

CHAPTER TWO

BREAKFAST

I am a breakfast person. I go to bed looking forward to my breakfast and my cup of coffee the next morning. I used to have a food column entirely dedicated to breakfast, written on the premise that breakfast isn't just the most important meal of the day, it is also the most awesome. I luxuriate in a quiet and calming breakfast, in a slow moment of appreciating the start of a new day and the silent rising of the sun. But, having kids modified things somewhat. It didn't make me any less fond of breakfast, but it made breakfast time undeniably less relaxed. It also made it stupendously more amusing. Our mornings start with yells, invitations to "play with me," and questions of "what's for breakfast?" Here are some answers.

A NOTE ON COFFEE

If we are being sticklers about categories, coffee should, perhaps, be found in the drinks section of a cookbook. But if we are being *serious* about categories, coffee obviously belongs with breakfast. There can be no breakfast if there is no coffee. If you have children and you somehow don't require coffee before you can even look at other humans much less form words in the morning, well then you have some sort of superpower. And you needn't impart it to me because I love coffee.

There is a variety of ways to go about making camp coffee. We almost always opt for a French press. You can get unbreakable ones for camping. Occasionally, we use a good old-fashioned percolator or pour over. I've heard good things about the AeroPress for making one cup of coffee at a time, but we literally would not survive off one cup of coffee at a time, so I can't say I've tried it myself. Whatever your coffee maker of choice, before you leave home, make sure you have all the pieces of it and *plenty* of coffee beans, preground to the level of coarseness your coffee method requires.

CHERRY-PECAN GRANOLA

Most of my history with granola has precisely nothing to do with camping, but humor me anyway. From age twelve to age twenty, I ate granola with yogurt for breakfast every. single. day. Yes, there were exceptions for holidays and travel, but the point is, I ate a lot of granola. I had strong opinions about granola: big clusters, no nuts, yes dried fruit, lightly spiced. In fact, I was fond enough of granola that during freshman year of college, my roommate and I stole one of the bulk serving bins of granola from the cafeteria so we could have a source of granola that was not closed in the middle of the night. (Hopefully, it's been long enough that the statute of limitations is up on that little moment of delinquency from an otherwise resolute rule-follower.) Then, I developed an oat allergy.

So, I don't eat granola anymore (sigh). But my family does. This recipe is tailored to my husband's granola preferences, and we know he has good taste because he married me. Make a batch of this granola at home and pack it in a jar or sealed container to bring with you to camp. You can serve it with yogurt or milk for breakfast, but it's also excellent sprinkled over cooked fruit for a dessert (see the caramelized apple crumble on page 164).

Ingredients

2 cups (200 g) rolled oats

1 ½ cups (156 g) roughly chopped raw pecans

½ teaspoon ground cinnamon

¼ teaspoon ground nutmeg

¼ teaspoon sea salt

¾ cup (241 g) maple syrup

3 tablespoons (45 ml) olive oil

1 teaspoon vanilla extract

1 ½ cups (180 g) dried cherries

Make It

1. Preheat the oven to 250°F (120°C, or gas mark ½).

2. In a large bowl, combine the oats, nuts, spices, and salt. Pour the maple syrup, oil, and vanilla extract over and toss well to coat—the best tool for mixing is your hands, even though you'll get stupendously sticky.

3. Spread out the mixture in a single layer on a rimmed baking sheet (it's helpful to line the baking sheet with parchment paper, but it's not necessary). Bake in the oven for 45–50 minutes, then remove from the oven and use a large spatula to flip the granola over in large pieces, trying to break it apart as little as possible (breakage is inevitable, so don't worry about some breakage. You're just trying to minimize it so you can have bigger clusters at the end.). Return the granola to the oven and bake for another 45–50 minutes or until it is completely dry and no longer chewy if you take a bite.

4. Remove from the oven and allow to cool completely. Then, break into the size clusters that you like best, mix with the dried cherries, and store in a sealed container for up to two weeks.

HOMEMADE STRAWBERRIES AND CREAM INSTANT OATMEAL

Unlike granola, I've always felt a bit blah about oatmeal. But there was one type of oatmeal that always piqued my interest when I was younger, and that was the strawberries and cream instant oatmeal that I was allowed to have when we were camping. As the eight-year-old gourmet that I was, I imagine I liked it because I liked sugar and strawberry flavoring. Here is a homemade version that does away with artificial flavorings but is still creamy, fruity, and fast to stir up in camp.

Ingredients

MAKE AHEAD

2 cups (200 g) rolled oats

2 tablespoons (14 g) ground flaxseeds

¼ vanilla bean

2 tablespoons (30 g) brown sugar

1 tablespoon (8 g) powdered milk

1 pinch salt

ASSEMBLY

½ cup (160 g) strawberry jam (try the jam recipe from page 46)

½ cup (38 g) sliced strawberries

¼ cup (60 ml) heavy cream (or sour cream)

Make It

HOME

1. Pulse the rolled oats and the flaxseeds in a blender or food processor about 8 times, chopping the oats into bits that are one-quarter to one-half their original size.

2. Cut the quarter vanilla bean in half lengthwise and scrape the seeds (the paste in the middle) into the brown sugar and rub them together to combine.

3. Stir the chopped oats and flax together with the vanilla-sugar, milk powder, and salt. Store in an airtight container for transporting to camp.

recipe continues

NOTE: You don't have to, but the instant oats will be even better if you toast your oats in the oven before chopping them in the food processor. Just spread them on a baking sheet and toast in a 350°F (180°C, or gas mark 4) oven for about 10 minutes.

In Camp

For each bowl of oatmeal, add ½ cup (110 g) of the oatmeal mixture into a
bowl with about 1 cup boiling water, stir, and allow to sit for a few minutes.
Stir 1 to 2 tablespoons (20 to 40 g) of strawberry jam into each serving,
top with sliced strawberries, and drizzle with cream (or add a dollop of
spoonful of sour cream) to taste.

ON MAKING OATMEAL FUN

Trail Memories from Kaitlin

If you don't have oatmeal lovers and are still intent on serving oatmeal for breakfast while camping, as my parents were when we went on childhood camping trips, then the goal is simply to get some of the breakfast to pass your kids' lips so that you can move on with your day's adventures. If the latter sounds like your family, then you have to do whatever it takes. My parents let us have chocolate chips on oatmeal when we were camping. We could have as many chocolate chips as we wanted as long as we would eat the oatmeal. I will share from personal experience that I quickly learned not to overdo it on the chocolate chips even though I am a lifelong chocolate lover. My own children are split on the oatmeal front. I have definitely been known to pack a good supply of chocolate chips to entice them to eat oatmeal while camping. At home, our family usually adds a bit of maple syrup for sweetness, some plain Greek yogurt for moisture and tang, and the person's choice of nuts and dried fruit. On trail, we usually bring some of the following for each day we plan to have oatmeal: brown sugar or maple syrup; dried cranberries or raisins; and nuts such as pecans, walnuts, or peanuts. I also like to add jam to my oatmeal, which I learned to do when I lived in Finland.

THE BEST FLUFFY PANCAKES

I grew up with Norwegian pancakes, which differ from American pancakes in a whole host of ways. To wit, they are not at all fluffy. They are thin and eggy, rather crepe-like, in fact. They are usually spread with jam. And, they are usually eaten for supper, not breakfast. Anyway, the only time we had American pancakes was when we were camping and my dad was cooking them. They were most definitely made from a mix. I never liked them much.

Many years later, I was writing a regular food column on breakfast, and I decided it was time to reintroduce myself to American pancakes with an eye toward finding a recipe I loved. After trying many, many pancakes, I came down in the yogurt pancake camp. A thick, whole milk yogurt makes the batter fantastically rich and tangy, yielding a fluffier and more flavorful pancake.

Ingredients

DRY INGREDIENTS

1½ cups (188 g) all-purpose flour

½ teaspoon salt

2 teaspoons baking powder

½ teaspoon baking soda

½ teaspoon cinnamon

WET INGREDIENTS

2 large eggs

2 cups (460 g) full-fat thick yogurt (Greek yogurt works particularly well)

¼ cup (50 g) sugar

1 teaspoon vanilla (if you haven't brought vanilla, you can omit this, but I do think it really adds to the flavor)

Butter for frying

Make It

AT HOME

Stir together all the dry ingredients until well combined and place them in an airtight container with a sealable lid or sturdy bag with a zip closure. It's a good idea to label your container with the name of the recipe (ask me how I know).

IN CAMP

1. In a mixing bowl, stir together the eggs, yogurt, sugar, and vanilla (if using) until smooth. Gently stir in the dry ingredients until just barely mixed in. Seriously! Stop while it is still lumpy! The fluffiest pancakes come from batter that has been mixed no more than is absolutely necessary.

2. Heat a cast-iron skillet or frying pan over medium-low heat. Add a good chunk of butter and let it melt and foam. Then, add plops of batter in approximately quarter-cup (61 g) scoops. Leave about 2 inches (5 cm) between each pancake, since they spread as they cook.

recipe continues

3. Cook the pancakes until lots of little bubbles appear across the top of the uncooked batter and their edges have begun to set, about 2 minutes. Then flip the pancakes and cook until golden brown on the second side, about another minute. Serve the hot pancakes immediately to the waiting campers. Repeat with the remaining batter, using more butter as necessary.

ON TOPPING PANCAKES

We have four people in our family, and when we are at home, we have four different breakfasts. That's simply not allowed when camping, but we still all differ from one another on how we want to top our pancakes. Some of us love a fruity pancake, but others can't stand it. Some of us drown our pancakes, like sorrows, in a flood of maple syrup. Others shudder at the stickiness of maple syrup. So, we provide options for toppings. Here is an assembly of our favorites:

- Maple syrup. Duh. Don't hesitate to smear on a pat of butter first. Do make sure you don't leave your seven-year-old entirely unsupervised with the maple syrup.

- Peanut butter. You can also ratchet things up and spread some peanut butter on your pancakes before drizzling them with maple syrup. I learned this from Kaitlin's family. Her dad's pancakes were *never* from a mix.

- Yogurt and jam. If you have some leftover yogurt that didn't go into the batter (which you likely do), spread your pancakes with some of the yogurt and then spoon jam on top.

- Fruit. I like my fruit cooked into my pancakes. I'll often scatter berries or slices of peach across the tops of my pancakes while the first side cooks. I then flip the pancakes, and the fruit caramelizes and bubbles into jammy pockets while the second side cooks. On the other hand, our younger son thinks cooked fruit is an affront and prefers his pancakes with lots of butter, raw fruit or berries, and definitely no syrup.

- Honey with either lots of butter or some ricotta cheese (I keep ricotta around for my pizzas) is also rather nice.

CORNMEAL CHORIZO PANCAKES

I can't actually remember the genesis of the idea for these pancakes, just that once upon a time I scrawled the words "cornmeal chorizo pancakes" in a notebook only to forget about it and finally rediscover it three years later. Upon rediscovery, I knew I had to create the actual recipe. The batter—based on a classic sour cream pancake batter—is loaded with sour cream and bound together with only as much flour and cornmeal as is absolutely necessary. These are some of our favorite pancakes. A bit like bacon, dried chorizo (*not* fresh, which is more like an Italian sausage; dried chorizo is more like a spiced salami) is really lovely with maple syrup. But, you can also play off the corn and spice and top your pancakes with smashed avocado and sea salt instead.

Ingredients

DRY INGREDIENTS

½ teaspoon fine sea salt

1 cup (126 g) fine cornmeal

½ cup (63 g) all-purpose flour

2 teaspoons (9 g) baking powder

½ teaspoon baking soda

WET INGREDIENTS

2 cups (460) sour cream

2 large eggs

2 tablespoons (40 g) maple syrup

1 cup (110 g) finely diced dried chorizo

Butter, for frying

TOPPINGS: either maple syrup (peaches are good too) or smashed avocado and sea salt

Make It

AT HOME

Mix the dry ingredients together, stirring to combine well, then seal in an airtight container with a sealable lid or a sturdy bag with a zip closure.

IN CAMP

1. Whisk together the sour cream, eggs, and maple syrup until smooth. Gently fold in the dry ingredients until two-thirds of the way mixed in, then add the chorizo bits and continue folding the ingredients together just until there are no dry streaks of flour. The batter should still be lumpy.

2. Heat a large cast-iron skillet or frying pan to medium heat. Add a large pat of butter and let it melt and foam. Add the batter in quarter-cup (58 g) spoonfuls, leaving space between the pancakes because they spread.

3. Cook the first side until bubbles appear across the batter, the edges appear dry, and they are a deep golden brown on the bottom, about 3 minutes. Flip and cook until the second side is golden brown, about a minute.

4. Serve the pancakes while warm with the topping(s) of your choice.

FRESH BERRY QUICK JAM

There's nothing not to like about freshly made jam. It tastes like love, like sweet, concentrated berry goodness. Kaitlin's family all share the same happiest camping memory, which includes their dad stopping by a farmer's market to buy berries when they were car camping in Nova Scotia and turning the berries into a quick jam. So there you have it: Jam makes happy memories. You can too.

This quick, fresh berry jam is really more of a compote, but it's also what I like to make because, well, it's quick. And in spite of romantic homesteading aspirations, I have never been good at canning.

Ingredients

½ pound (227 g) fresh berries of any sort, hulled and quartered if needed

½ cup (100 g) sugar

A squeeze of lemon juice (optional, but it helps the jam set)

Make It

1. Combine the berries and sugar in a small pot and bring to a simmer, covered.

2. Once simmering, turn the heat down to low and begin smashing the berries up with a fork as they soften. Cook uncovered until slightly thickened, about 10 minutes.

3. Stir in the lemon juice, if you're using it. Serve warm or cool.

NORWEGIAN PANCAKES, AKA *PANNEKAKER*

Ahhhh, pancakes as I know them. The most delicious, tender, lacy, and buttery morsels. As I have mentioned, Norwegian pancakes are thin and crepe-like, which can make them a little intimidating to flip. But, believe in yourself like I believe in you and great things are possible. For example, pancakes.

Ingredients

1⅓ cups (167 g) all-purpose flour

6 large eggs

½ teaspoon salt

3 tablespoons (39 g) sugar

1 teaspoon ground cardamom or lemon zest, whichever you prefer (which obviously means cardamom)

3 cups (710 ml) whole milk

4 tablespoons (55 g) butter, melted, plus more for greasing the pan

Jam and butter for serving

Make It

1. In a large bowl, whisk together the flour, eggs, salt, sugar, and cardamom or lemon zest until the mixture is thick and yellow.

2. Bit by bit, whisk in the milk to make a smooth batter. Allow to rest for half an hour. (I don't actually know what this does to the batter, but it is simply something you "must do.")

3. Right before frying the pancakes, whisk the melted butter into the batter.

4. Heat a 9- or 12-inch (23 or 30 cm) skillet (I like cast iron best) over medium-high heat. Melt a bit of butter in it, then pour in a ladle full of batter and swirl it around to coat the bottom of the pan. It should be about the thickness of a crepe or just slightly thicker.

5. Cook for about 2 minutes until the underside has turned golden brown and the top is beginning to set. Then flip it (this can be tricky, and the first one almost always gets ruined) and cook the other side for just a minute. Transfer to a serving plate.

6. Grease the pan with a little more butter and continue frying up the batter until it is all used. You should use pretty high heat the whole time, but if the pancakes start burning and the pan starts smoking, turn the heat down a bit.

7. Serve the pancakes with butter and jam. To serve, you spread a pancake with butter and jam, then roll it up like a jellyroll and slice and eat it.

QUICK RICE PORRIDGE

In leftover rice we trust. Leftover rice is not so much leftovers as it is an important ingredient for starting a new meal. Make extra rice at dinner one night so you can have fried rice the next day (page 94) or this soft and comforting rice porridge for breakfast. I like to sweeten my porridge with maple syrup and spice it with cardamom and cinnamon. Sometimes I add raisins, or sometimes I sprinkle berries on top, but really you can do whatever you want. A nice thing about this porridge is that it works more as a template than a recipe. You can swap in coconut milk or macadamia nut milk for the dairy, for example, and you can use any type of leftover rice (just know that different rice will yield different textures). Our senior year in college, Kaitlin and I had an apartment together, and we were famous for serving our wild rice version of this porridge for breakfast. It was a mix of wild rice, cream, dried cranberries and blueberries, and maple syrup. Whenever we had visitors, we would force them to wake up at 5:30 in the morning to eat it with us before we headed out for our days—unforgettable for a variety of reasons.

Ingredients

2 cups (440 g) leftover cooked rice

1–2 cups (237–475 ml) whole milk, cream, or coconut milk

2 tablespoons (20 g) maple syrup (use more or less to taste)

1 teaspoon ground cinnamon

1 teaspoon ground cardamom

A couple pinches of salt

Dried or fresh fruit for topping

Make It

1. Combine the rice, dairy (or coconut milk), maple syrup, spices, and salt in a pot. Warm over medium heat until the mixture almost reaches a simmer. Turn the heat to low and cook, stirring quite a lot so the milk doesn't scorch the bottom of the pan, until the rice has absorbed much of the milk and you have a spoonable, porridgy texture. This usually takes 7–10 minutes.

2. Divide the porridge into bowls and top with fruit and more maple syrup, if desired. Rice porridge is good warm or cold, so if any kids with you tend to lose focus while eating and decide to run off and collect some really special rocks or really good sticks, their porridge will still be good when they make their way back to it.

THE BEST SIMPLE EGG SANDWICHES, TWO WAYS

Over the years, I have pursued creativity and wild variety in my breakfast sandwiches. I spent years on a veritable breakfast sandwich *rumspringe*, seeking out everything that could possibly go on an English muffin—or bagel, or croissant, or toast—with an egg. All this sandwiching has finally brought me to the surprising yet perhaps inevitable conclusion that simple breakfast sandwiches are the best. My favorite breakfast sandwich is so simple, it doesn't even involve bacon. But, where it diverges from a more standard breakfast sandwich is that I like sharp cheddar. I like the tang against the mildness of an egg. I also like to swiftly wilt some spinach with garlic and add that in. My kids don't. They like mild cheddar. And egg. And that's it. So, I make both versions. But, everybody gets their egg "frambled," a fun combination of scrambled and fried that I discovered when all my egg cooking was done one-handed because the other arm was always holding a baby. It's a technique that I've actually seen used by some chefs, so I feel validated. It gives an almost omelet-like texture that works quite well in a breakfast sandwich. This recipe makes two "grown-up" sandwiches and two "kid" sandwiches. But feel free to eat either kind!

Ingredients

Butter

4 English muffins, split open

2 slices mild cheddar cheese

2 slices sharp cheddar cheese

4 eggs

1 small clove of garlic, minced

2 cups (60 g) baby spinach leaves

Salt and pepper

Hot sauce for serving (optional)

Make It

1. Heat a large cast-iron skillet either on your cook stove or over the fire at medium-high heat. Butter the insides of the English muffins and place them face down in the skillet. Cook for 2–3 minutes until they are golden brown, flip them over, and cook the second sides until lightly browned, another 2–3 minutes. Transfer each English muffin to a plate. Place a slice of cheese on one half of each of the English muffins (so two of the muffins get sharp cheddar, and two get mild).

recipe continues

2. Return the pan to the heat and add a big knob of butter. Allow the butter to melt, then crack in the four eggs. Sprinkle each egg with salt and pepper and use a wooden spoon to swirl the yolk and white of each egg together to be somewhat marbled looking but not fully scrambled. Cook for a little less than a minute, allowing the bottoms to set. Give the eggs a few little extra swirls with the spoon to achieve the desired amount of yolk-white marbling. Use the spoon to break the eggs apart from each other, then flip them over and allow the second sides to cook until set but not browned, another 15 seconds or so. Transfer each egg to one of the cheese-topped English muffin halves.

3. Add the tops to the two sandwiches with the mild cheddar. At the same time, add another pat of butter to the skillet over medium-high heat and add the minced garlic. Let the garlic sizzle for about 30 seconds, then stir in the spinach and a big pinch of salt. Stir until the spinach is wilted and coated with butter, usually just a few seconds. Divide the hot spinach between the two sharp cheddar breakfast sandwiches, then close these up. Serve with hot sauce on the side.

HASH BROWN BREAKFAST BURRITOS

My world was forever changed by breakfast burritos we ate in Lake Tahoe. It may have been the fresh air that made them taste so good. Or the fresh pico de gallo. But there is also something deeply satisfying about hash browns wrapped in a tortilla.

You could bring everything and make these fresh in camp, but it also works well to make them at home, wrap them tightly in foil, freeze them, and then reheat them in camp over the fire—a burrito technique I learned from my favorite ten-year-old, Gigi. Make the pico de gallo while they reheat.

Ingredients

BREAKFAST BURRITOS

½ pound (227 g) bacon

¾ pound (340 g) hash browns

8 eggs

1 ½ cups (173 g) shredded mild cheddar cheese

Salt and pepper

6 large taco-sized (but not burrito-sized) flour tortillas

Olive oil and butter, as needed

PICO DE GALLO

2 medium ripe tomatoes

½ cup (80 g) finely chopped red onion

½ jalapeño pepper, seeds removed, finely diced

¼ cup (4 g) chopped fresh cilantro

Juice of one small lime

Salt

Make It

TO MAKE THE BURRITOS

1. Slice the bacon into small bits and fry in a hot frying pan until crispy, about 4–7 minutes. Use a slotted spoon to transfer the bacon bits to a plate lined with a paper towel.

2. Pour off all but 2 tablespoons (30 ml) of the bacon oil from the frying pan, add the hash browns, and press into a single layer. Sprinkle lightly with salt. Cook over medium-high heat until the bottom of the potato layer is all brown and crispy, about 5–7 minutes. Drizzle the top with olive oil, then flip the potato layer over in sections and continue cooking until the potato pieces are brown and crispy, another 5 minutes or so. Add more oil as needed. Transfer to a plate.

3. Return the frying pan to medium-low heat and add a pat of butter. Crack in your eggs, sprinkle with salt, and start stirring with a wooden spoon. Cook, stirring constantly until the eggs are softly set. Stir the cheese into the eggs, then remove from the heat.

recipe continues

4. If you are serving the burritos right away, simply divide the hash browns, eggs, and bacon bits between the tortillas, roll up the burritos, and serve with pico de gallo.

5. To make ahead, let all the ingredients come to room temperature, then divide the ingredients between the tortillas, fold in the tops and bottoms, and roll them tightly into burritos. Then, wrap each burrito in foil and freeze. Before packing into your cooler, place all the wrapped, frozen burritos in a heavy-duty zip-top plastic bag or a sealable container. Allow the burritos to defrost before reheating. To reheat, heat a cast-iron skillet (or other heavy skillet) on a grate over the campfire or camp stove and place the burritos, still wrapped in foil, into the skillet a few at a time. Heat for 3–4 minutes per side or until warmed through, then transfer to plates, unwrap, and enjoy with pico de gallo.

MAKES 1 ½ CUPS (270 G)

TO MAKE THE PICO DE GALLO

Stir all the ingredients together and season with salt to taste. You can serve the pico de gallo right away, but it gets more flavorful as it sits, so feel free to make it a couple hours or a day ahead and store in a sealed container.

DUTCH OVEN COFFEE CAKE

This "coffee cake" is actually based on a classic French yogurt cake. Yogurt cake is such a simple and delicious recipe that it's one of the first things most French children learn to cook, using the yogurt cup as their only measuring tool. I've added raspberries and a streusel topping to take it more in a classic coffee cake direction because I can resist neither streusel nor jammy pockets of berries. But really, it's like adding a statement necklace to a classic white button-up; it's excellent with or without.

Ingredients

FOR THE CAKE

Butter for greasing the Dutch oven

1½ cups (188 g) flour

2 teaspoons baking powder

¾ teaspoon salt

1 cup (200 g) sugar

¾ cup (180 g) whole milk yogurt (preferably Greek yogurt)

½ cup (118 ml) vegetable oil

2 eggs

1½ teaspoons vanilla extract

2 cups (250 g) fresh raspberries

FOR THE STREUSEL

½ cup (100 g) sugar

⅓ cup (42 g) flour

1 teaspoon ground cinnamon

¼ cup butter (55 g), softened

SPECIAL EQUIPMENT: a 10-inch (25 cm) Dutch oven

Make It

1. Grease your Dutch oven well with butter, and if desired, you can line it with parchment paper.

2. Combine the flour, baking powder, and salt in a small bowl and set aside. This step can be done at home. Simply transfer the mixture to a sealed container, label it "coffee cake dry ingredients," and pack.

3. In a bowl, whisk together the sugar, yogurt, vegetable oil, eggs, and vanilla extract until entirely blended. Stir in the dry ingredients until just combined, then fold in the raspberries. This is a great mixing project for the kids!

4. Pour the batter into the Dutch oven. In the bowl that held the dry ingredients, rub together the streusel ingredients until they are crumbly. Sprinkle this over the cake batter.

5. Place the lid on the Dutch oven and either set it on a grate over coals or create a ring of coals on a heat-resistant surface and set the Dutch oven directly on top. Shovel more coals onto the top of the Dutch oven. Allow the cake to bake until a knife inserted into it comes out clean, around 40 minutes. You will have to add new hot coals to the lid and bottom 1–2 times during this baking time. (For more specific directions on Dutch oven cooking, refer to the "Dutch Oven Primer," page 25.) When the cake is done, carefully take it off the heat, remove the lid, and allow the cake to cool for at least 10 minutes before serving.

SKILLET BISCUITS

A confession for you: I adore Pillsbury biscuits. The kind you pop out of a tube. The kind that have such perfect layers you just know that they could only be achieved by science. I am fully aware they have lots of weird ingredients in them that I would normally never eat, but I have been known to stash a tube in our cooler and then cook them in a cast-iron skillet over the campfire for a camping breakfast. But, I got to thinking, wouldn't everyone win if I figured out how to do the same with made-from-scratch biscuits?

I turned, almost immediately, to my other favorite biscuits, which are the nearly infallible cream biscuits from America's Test Kitchen. The dough for these biscuits is a little less delicate and can be worked a bit more than buttermilk biscuits, making them better for camping conditions. They are wildly simple. And, like I said, they are nearly infallible. As long as you keep the heat at a moderate temperature, they griddle up beautifully. There's only one wee catch: The dough has to be griddled immediately. This means that if you are using a skillet that can't hold eight biscuits at once, mix one half-batch, and while the first four biscuits are cooking on their second side, mix up the second half-batch.

Ingredients

2 cups (250 g) all-purpose flour

2 teaspoons sugar

2 teaspoons baking powder

½ teaspoon salt

1½ cups (355 ml) heavy cream

Make It

AT HOME

Mix the dry ingredients together in a sealed container. Label it "biscuit mix."

IN CAMP

1. Place a cast-iron skillet on a grate over your campfire over an area of medium-low heat (you could also use your camp stove over low-medium heat) and allow it to heat for about 5 minutes. While the skillet heats, place the dry ingredients in a bowl, make a well in the center, and pour in the cream. Stir it until the dough has come together in a shaggy ball. Then knead the dough ball in the bowl, working in any flour that hasn't been incorporated, for about 8–10 turns of the dough until it's just a bit smoother.

recipe continues

TRAIL MEMORY

This biscuit recipe and skillet methodology recalls bannock, an old-school camping bread that many people still enjoy making. Our neighbor Sherry (Kaitlin's mom) shared many excerpts from old recipe notecards and books from Wilderness Canoe Base with me, and the notes on the recipe for bannock made me giggle. "Famous open fires trail bread," the recipe card trumpets. And the end of the recipe reads, "Test with a stick to make sure it is done in the middle. If it isn't it will probably still taste good. Campers are hungry!"

2. Divide the dough into eight equal(ish) pieces and flatten each piece into a circle a little less than ¾ inch (2 cm) thick. Transfer all the biscuits to the heated skillet, cover, and cook until they are nicely browned, about 7 minutes. Flip the biscuits, cover the skillet again, and cook until they are browned and cooked through, approximately 7 more minutes.

3. Transfer the biscuits to a plate and let them sit for 5 minutes before eating to make sure the middles finish. Eat warm with jam or alongside eggs. These taste so much better when they are freshly cooked, so eat up!

DUTCH OVEN SWEET ROLLS

Let me be perfectly honest and say Dutch oven sweet rolls are not a normal part of our breakfast rotation. Enriched dough is a commitment, assembling cinnamon rolls is a commitment, yeasted dough baking in a Dutch oven is a commitment . . . That's a lot of commitment. But, when we were talking about the best recipes to go in this book, my friend Kaitlin said, and I quote, "My parents swear they used to make yeast sweet rolls on trail on layover days. I'm not sure if I actually believe them."

So, of course then I had to go talk to Kaitlin's parents. Mark and Sherry insisted that they did indeed make sweet rolls and all sorts of yeasted breads on trail when they were canoe guides. Sherry said Mark would canoe with dough rising in a container under his seat so that he could bake in camp while she would only bake yeast rolls on layover days. Naturally, I took all of this as a challenge to make my own Dutch oven sweet rolls. And let me tell you, it was easier than I thought, worked better than I expected, and was absolutely delicious. It took commitment, to be sure, but sometimes commitment is a good thing.

Ingredients

1½ cups water (118 ml), just slightly warm to the touch

1 teaspoon active dry yeast

2 tablespoons (26 g) sugar

3½ cups (438 g) flour, plus more for rolling

1 teaspoon salt

1 teaspoon orange zest

⅓ cup (79 ml) olive oil

¼ cup butter (56 g), very soft

½ cup (115 g) brown sugar

2 teaspoons ground cinnamon

¼ cup (80 g) maple syrup

SPECIAL EQUIPMENT: a 9-inch (23 cm) metal cake pan or aluminum pie plate and a 10-inch (25 cm) Dutch oven

Make It

AT HOME

1. In the bowl of an electric mixer with a bread hook, combine the water, yeast, and sugar. Let stand until the yeast foams up, about 5–10 minutes.

2. Add half the flour and the salt to the mixing bowl. Turn the mixer to low and mix while adding the remaining flour. When all the flour is incorporated and the dough is shaggy, add the orange zest and drizzle in the olive oil along the edge of the bowl. Add another tablespoon or two of flour to help incorporate the olive oil into the dough. Turn the mixer to medium-low and let the bread hook knead until the dough is elastic and smooth, about 5 minutes. You want the dough to be smooth and satiny but still slightly tacky to the touch, but if it is really sticky, add more flour a little at a time until it pulls away from the sides and kneads into a ball. Kneading can also be done by hand for 8–10 minutes.

3. Turn the dough out into a large, oiled bowl, cover with plastic wrap or a damp kitchen towel, and allow it to rise until doubled in size, about 2 hours.

recipe continues

4. When the dough is pillowy and fully risen, turn it out onto a lightly floured surface. Roll the dough out into a rectangle that's about 18 inches (45.5 cm) long and 14–16 inches (35.5–40.5 cm) wide. Spread the softened butter onto the dough, then sprinkle the brown sugar and cinnamon evenly across it. Start from the shorter edge and roll into a jellyroll, rolling tightly enough that there aren't any gaps or air pockets but not too tight because then the dough may not expand as much during its second rise. Using a sharp knife or a bench scraper, divide the roll into eight pieces.

5. Butter your cake pan or pie tin well and arrange the unbaked rolls in it. The rolls will have space between them, which is fine because they will poof up as they rise and poof even more as they bake. At this point, cover the dish tightly and refrigerate it or freeze it before packing it into your cooler to bring to camp.

AT CAMP

1. When you are ready to bake, allow the rolls to thaw if they are frozen. Place the dish of cold rolls in a warm place or near your fire until they have risen and are puffy and pillowy, about an hour. Let your fire burn to hot embers. Place the cake pan or pie tin with the rolls inside your Dutch oven. Cover the Dutch oven, then place it on a grate over the hot embers or make a ring of hot embers on a heat-resistant surface and place the Dutch oven directly on top. Shovel coals and embers on top of your Dutch oven. Allow the rolls to bake until they are fully cooked through but still soft toward the center. You will need to replenish the hot coals on the top and bottom of the Dutch oven a couple of times while baking. (For more specific directions on Dutch oven cooking, refer to the "Dutch Oven Primer," page 25.)

2. When the rolls are cooked through, remove them from the heat, remove the lid of the Dutch oven, and drizzle maple syrup all over the tops of the hot rolls. Allow the rolls to cool enough to handle, then serve warm, sticky, and delicious.

FRITTATA

Frittatas are the Statue of Liberty of food: "Give me your tired, your wilted, your leftover vegetables, and I will make them into a meal." A pan full of fluffy eggs with assorted vegetables and cheeses and meats is as flexible as it is filling and delicious. I like almost anything in a frittata (especially bitter greens or melted leeks and lemon), but my boys like their eggs as plain as possible, so we have learned to meet in the middle with mild zucchini and punchy—but child-friendly in its salty creaminess—feta.

Ingredients

2 tablespoons (30 ml) olive oil

1 small yellow onion, chopped

1 medium-large zucchini, sliced into rounds

8 eggs

¾ teaspoon salt, divided

½ cup (75 g) crumbled feta cheese

Make It

1. In a heavy bottomed 9-inch (23 cm) skillet, heat the olive oil over medium-high heat until it shimmers. Add the onion and cook until it has softened and become translucent, then add the zucchini. Cook, stirring occasionally, until the zucchini is soft, about 8–10 minutes. In general, the zucchini will go through stages where first it is dry and seems to soak up all the oil, then it will release all of its liquid and everything will seem soggy and watery, and then as the liquid simmers off, the zucchini will soften and brown. When the zucchini is soft, stir in ¼ teaspoon salt.

2. Meanwhile, in a medium bowl whisk the eggs with the remaining salt. When the zucchini has softened, pour the eggs over the zucchini and sprinkle the feta on top. Turn the heat down to medium-low and cover the pan. Cook until the eggs have cooked through and just set on top, 6–8 minutes.

CHILAQUILES

Can there be a greater endorsement for a dish than "it's chips and salsa for breakfast"? I think not. Chilaquiles, a traditional Mexican dish, is fundamentally fried tortillas coated in a brothy salsa. But for camping, you can use store-bought salsa and chips to make chilaquiles that are ready in a matter of moments! Topped with a fried egg, avocado slices, and fresh cheese, this is the most perfectly satisfying start to any day. But, it also makes a great speedy dinner, and you can easily swap out toppings for other favorites (think meats, beans, or veggies)!

Ingredients

2 cups (520 g) store-bought salsa (tomato or tomatillo, depending on if you prefer chilaquiles rojos or verdes!), at whatever level of spiciness your family likes

¼ cup (60 ml) water

8 cups (208 g) tortilla chips

1 tablespoon (14 g) butter

4 eggs

Salt

Avocado slices, queso fresco, and cilantro for serving (optional)

Make It

1. In a large skillet over medium-high heat, bring the salsa to a simmer. Stir in the water to loosen the salsa, then simmer for about 2 minutes.

2. Add the tortilla chips and stir well to coat, then cook until the chips are warmed through, 2–3 minutes. Transfer the chilaquiles to plates.

3. Return the pan to the heat and add the butter. When the butter has melted and foamed, crack in the eggs. Sprinkle with salt. Fry the eggs to your desired level of doneness, then slide an egg onto each plate of chilaquiles.

4. Add avocado, queso fresco, and cilantro (or other toppings!) as desired.

EGGS IN PURGATORY

There's something about the combination of eggs and tomatoes that just *works*. The duo can be enjoyed in a variety of ways, but the evocatively named Italian dish *uova al purgatorio*, eggs in purgatory, is one of the simplest. It's also my favorite. Here's my little secret: While most renditions of eggs in purgatory call for you to whip up a tomato sauce before nestling in the eggs to simmer, I most often make this dish with leftover pizza sauce because we only use a small portion of a jar when we make pizza. This makes it into a super speedy 5-minute dish that is still wonderfully delicious. Depending on what region of Italy you are in, eggs cooked in tomato sauce can be mild or quite spicy. I keep ours mild (I introduced our kids to spicy food as soon as they could eat, and they still never took to it! Maybe it's an unavoidable side effect of growing up in Minnesota??), but if you and yours want a kick, throw in some red pepper flakes.

Ingredients

About 2 cups (490 g) of leftover pizza sauce or marinara sauce

¼ cup (60 ml) water

6 eggs

Salt and pepper

Fresh basil or parsley, chopped (optional)

Toasted bread for serving (*not* optional)

Make It

1. In a skillet, bring the tomato sauce and the quarter cup water to a boil. Turn down the heat to a simmer and crack the eggs into the sauce. Sprinkle each egg with salt and pepper. Cover the pan and cook over low until the whites are completely set and the yolks are as set as you like them, about 3–5 minutes. By all rights, you should just cook the eggs until the yolks are hot but still runny. However, all the members of our household under the age of eight insist they do not like runny yolks, so I let theirs cook longer. I know that I am right and they are wrong, but I didn't like runny yolks at their age either. I did see the light by the time I was in early high school, so I trust they will come around on their own.

2. Scoop the cooked eggs and sauce onto plates, sprinkle with herbs (if using), and serve with toasted bread.

CHAPTER THREE

LUNCHES
and Foods on the Go

Sandwiches are one of the most satisfying meals. All I ever really want to eat for lunch is a sandwich. But guess what I almost never eat? Yeah, sandwiches. My role in our family is leftover patrol, so my lunches are almost always an assortment of odds and ends. But not when camping. It's sandwiches, baby!!!! However, let me tell you a very important truth about sandwiches (I'll wait while you go get your notebook to write this down): The difference between a good sandwich and a bad sandwich lies entirely in the quality of the ingredients.

That's right. It's not in the creative combination of flavors. You can have a sandwich as simple as bread, butter, and ham; it doesn't sound like much, but if you have a good baguette, thickly spread salted European butter, and lacy, fatty slices of the best ham,

you'll have an edible, portable piece of paradise. So, when you are shopping, choose good bread and good-quality meats and cheeses. Okay, thank you for attending my seminar on sandwiches. Now let's make some!

NOTE: Since this chapter is technically not 100 percent about sandwiches, I have also included a handful of lunches that aren't sandwiches, in case that's what your family likes best. You'll also find an assortment of packable snacks, because sometimes—oftentimes—a tasty morsel of bribery is needed to keep short legs moving along a rocky and rooted path.

CLASSIC CAMPING SANDWICH

Other than peanut butter and jelly, this is the sandwich I most associate with camping. The first time I ever went camping with *no* adults(!), my friends and I used one of our dad's packing lists to guide our preparation. We followed it to the letter, which meant the only lunch options we had packed were tortillas with peanut butter and jelly (that we had transferred into portable camping tubes proffered by the dads) and these summer sausage and cheese sandwiches. It was fantastic.

Ingredients

2 slices of really good, crusty whole-grain bread

2–3 ounces (55–85 g) mild cheddar (or a mild creamy cheese such as muenster, otherwise known to our family as "monster cheese," is also good)

2 ounces (55 g) sliced summer sausage

Make It

Layer the cheese and sausage on one slice of bread and top with the other. If you want a really excellent sandwich experience, add mayo, mustard, and lettuce. If you want a really authentic sandwich experience, bread, cheese, and sausage it is! I can't really say it better than my friend Haakon: "When I'm at home, summer sausage never sounds that good. But when I'm camping, I just really want summer sausage."

CURRIED TUNA SALAD

This changed everything about tuna salad for me. It's the only kind I'll eat anymore. There's something transformative about the combination of curry powder and tuna—it's unexpected (versus chicken salad, for example, where you kind of do expect it) but familiar at the same time. And it's straight-up good. The idea comes from a sandwich at Flour Bakery in Boston, but I've tidied up the frills to make it suitable for making in camp—though if it sounds good, do feel free to try it at home! As with much of the food in this book, I sure do.

Ingredients

2 cans or pouches of tuna (drained, if cans)

¼ cup (60 g) mayonnaise

2 teaspoons (4 g) curry powder

Squeeze of lemon juice

2 tablespoons (18 g) golden raisins

Make It

1. Stir together the tuna, mayonnaise, curry powder, and lemon juice until well mixed. Then stir in the raisins.

2. Serve on ciabatta with very ripe tomato slices and arugula. Serve as an open-faced sandwich on a slice of bread with avocado. Serve on celery sticks. Serve on nori sheets (I know, it sounds weird, but you don't know until you've tried it).

NORWEGIAN *MATPAKKE*

Hold tight because I'm about to dump you into the middle of an ongoing marital dispute. By way of important context, my mom is from Norway, and I grew up spending all of my summers in Norway. In Norway, both breakfasts and lunches tend to be an open-faced sandwich, a simple slice of bread with butter and either cheese or meat (occasionally both), plus a couple of vegetable slices. If you will be having lunch on the go, you make a *matpakke*—literally a "food pack"—toward the end of eating breakfast. When you're Norwegian, there are strict rules about the "right" way to do things, and this goes for making a *matpakke* as much as for anything else. You make yourself two open-faced sandwiches, then you stack them—face to face—and wrap them in paper to transport them. My husband insists, repeatedly and volubly, that these stacked open-faced sandwiches are "just a sandwich" and that it is unreasonable to say otherwise. He is wrong. It is a *matpakke*. It is two open-faced sandwiches, and you must disassemble them before eating them!

Ingredients

2 slices of good, crusty whole-grain bread

European butter

1–2 ounces (28–55 g) Jarlsberg cheese, thinly sliced

1–2 slices red bell pepper

About 4 thin slices of good salami

A few very thin slices of cucumber

Make It

1. Butter each slice of bread well, then top one of them with Jarlsberg and red pepper and the other with salami and cucumber. Put the two pieces of bread together as if you were making it all into a sandwich, but be aware, this is *not* a sandwich. It is a *matpakke*.

2. Wrap up your not-a-sandwich in brown paper or in a sealed container to bring with you wherever the morning may take you. To serve, take the two halves apart again so you have one open-faced sandwich with cheese and pepper and one with salami and cucumber. This is important because there is a right way and a wrong way to do things, and Norwegians do it the right way!

FARMER'S LUNCH SANDWICH

This is one of my all-time favorite sandwiches inspired by a sandwich from my neighborhood café and grocer when I lived in Boston. The simplicity of the Farmer's Lunch sandwich is deceiving—it tastes like *so* much more than the sum of its parts. The sharp cheese, the sweet-tart apple, and the brine of the pickles with the mayo and mustard all thrum together like a symphony. This is what I make for myself when my kiddos just want cheese sandwiches with apple slices on the side.

Ingredients

¼ of a nice, crusty baguette, sliced in half horizontally

1 tablespoon (14 g) good mayonnaise

1 tablespoon (11 g) grainy mustard

3–4 ounces (85–115 g) really sharp cheddar cheese, sliced

¼ tart apple (such as Granny Smith), cut into thin slices

5–6 slices of bread and butter pickle (or pickled green tomatoes if you can get them)

One large leaf of lettuce (optional)

Make It

1. Smear each side of the baguette with half the mayo and half the mustard. I like this sandwich to be heavy on the condiments (much to the chagrin of some of our family members who are scared of condiments), but you can adjust the amount you use to suit your taste.

2. On the bottom half of the baguette, layer on the cheese, apple slices, and pickle slices, then add the lettuce if using.

3. Cover with the top half of the baguette. Enjoy!

SMOKED SALMON AND BAGEL SANDWICH

Salmon and cream cheese bagels are not just for eating as you walk from your subway stop to work in New York City. In fact, this salmon bagel is an entirely different beast with hot smoked salmon instead of lox and scallions instead of red onions and capers. But, like its big-city counterpart, it is delicious and surprisingly amenable to being a meal on the go.

Ingredients

1 bagel, sliced in half (I never toast my bagels, but if you prefer toasted, you will have to toast it in a pan or over the fire ahead of time)

1–2 ounces (28–55 g) cream cheese

1 tablespoon (6 g) sliced scallions

1–2 ounces (28–55 g) hot smoked salmon (the kind that is flaky and opaque, not the translucent soft kind that is cold smoked salmon or lox)

Lettuce and sliced tomato (optional but yummy)

Make It

1. Spread cream cheese on both halves of the bagel.

2. Sprinkle half the scallion slices on each bagel half and press them into the cream cheese.

3. Layer the smoked salmon (and lettuce and tomato, if using) on the bottom half of the bagel. Cover with the other half and enjoy.

SMILING PEANUT BUTTER RICE CAKES

This lunch or snack ticks basically every box for family camping food. Easy? Check. Kid-friendly? Check. Packed with energy? Check. Doesn't need refrigeration? Check. Fun to assemble? Check. Healthy? Check. Guess you had better make them!

Ingredients

4 rice cakes

¼ cup (65 g) peanut butter

1 apple, cored and cut into 8 slices

Raisins

Cinnamon (optional)

Make It

1. Spread each rice cake with a tablespoon (16 g) of peanut butter.

2. Use apple slices and raisins to make smiling faces on the peanut butter rice cakes. Then watch your children pile on many, many more raisins.

3. If desired, sprinkle with cinnamon before serving.

RYE CRISPS WITH HARD-BOILED EGG

We ate absolute boatloads of Wasa rye crisps growing up. In Norwegian, they are called *knekkebrød*, but my brothers always called them *knekke-blur*. It makes sense since they disappeared so fast! Their cracker-like crunch gives a fun lift to any and all sorts of toppings (we often use the same toppings as in a *matpakke*, page 77), but they are at their very best when they act as a foil for creamy things. Enter avocado and hard-boiled eggs, two of my sons' favorite foods, and you have an absolutely smashing lunch. I add pickled red onion to perk up mine and cut through all the richness with a briny punch. If you have the eggs already boiled and a small, sealed container of pickled onions, all you need is a knife and an appetite.

Ingredients

2 rye crisp breads

Butter

One half of an avocado

Salt

1 hardboiled egg (made ahead of time, see below for recipe)

About 6 pieces of pickled red onion (optional; made at home, recipe follows)

Make It

1. Spread each rye crisp with a thick layer of butter, mash on the avocado, then sprinkle with a pinch of salt. Peel the hardboiled egg (you can do this ahead of time and transport the peeled hardboiled egg in a sealed container) and slice it into ¼- to ½-inch (0.5–1 cm) thick slices.

2. Layer the slices on top of the avocado and sprinkle with another pinch of salt. Top each crisp with a forkful of pickled red onions, if you're using them, which you should be because they are particularly lovely in this application.

HARD-BOILED EGG

To cook eggs ahead of time, bring a small pot of water to a boil, add as many eggs as you wish, and cook for 6–8 minutes depending on how hard cooked you like them. Cook for 6 minutes for a more velvety yolk, 8 minutes for a fully set yolk. Once cooked, transfer to cold water to cool before you peel them. Transport them in a sealable container.

SERVES 1

QUICK PICKLED RED ONIONS

Ingredients

½ cup (120 ml) apple cider vinegar

½ cup (120 ml) water

1 tablespoon (18 g) coarse salt (use ½ tablespoon [4.5 g] if you're using regular table salt)

½ tablespoon (7 g) sugar

1 red onion, peeled and thinly sliced

Make It

1. In a small saucepan, heat the vinegar and water to a simmer. Stir in the salt and sugar until fully dissolved. Pour into a small bowl and add the onions, tossing them with the vinegar mixture until well coated. Let them stand at least 30 minutes, tossing them again, now and then, before using.

2. Once cool, store the onions in a covered container or jar in the refrigerator for several weeks. Seal some tightly in a jar and bring them in your cooler or backpack to use as a topping on everything from sandwiches to tacos to fried rice. They're one of the best edible bits of flair ever.

TURKEY AND GUACAMOLE WRAP

This may sound like just another turkey and guacamole wrap, but I assure you it is not. It is a turkey and guacamole wrap with *pizzazz!* The extra oomph comes from a hefty dose of mayonnaise and black pepper. And while using both mayonnaise *and* guacamole may seem like a little much in the condiment department, trust me when I say it's worth it. The spice, tang, and creaminess give deli turkey new life. Plus you're camping, so you deserve it.

Ingredients

1 large tortilla

2 tablespoons (28 g) mayonnaise

A generous sprinkling of ground black pepper

3 tablespoons (42 g) guacamole

About ¼ pound (115 g) shaved or sliced turkey breast

2–3 slices of ripe tomato

A small handful of arugula leaves (or other lettuce, but arugula's peppery flavor is nice here)

Make It

1. Spread the mayonnaise on the tortilla, then sprinkle it with a generous amount of black pepper. Spread on the guacamole, then top with the turkey. Add the tomato slices and arugula.

2. Fold the bottom and top in, then roll up the wrap like a burrito. Wrap tightly in parchment or wax paper or place in an airtight sandwich container to transport. Or eat it right away!

APRICOT-CHERRY-PISTACHIO BITES

I've been told these little fruit and nut bites are "addictively delicious." They're a bit like fruit and nut energy bars, except round, which is obviously more fun because it's kind of like edible polka dots.

Ingredients

1 cup (130 g) dried apricots

1 cup (120 g) dried cherries

1 cup (123 g) toasted, shelled pistachios

1 tablespoon (20 g) honey

1 teaspoon lemon zest

½ cup (42 g) toasted, shredded coconut (or sesame seeds), for rolling

Make It

1. Combine the apricots, cherries, pistachios, honey, and lemon zest in a food processor. Pulse/run the processor until everything is very finely chopped together but not turned into a paste—it takes a minute or so.

2. Line a baking sheet with parchment paper and put the coconut (or sesame seeds) in a small bowl. Roll a tablespoonful (6 g) of the mixture at a time into balls and roll the balls in the coconut (or sesame seeds) to coat, then place them on the baking sheet. Put the finished bites into the fridge to firm up for 1 hour.

3. After they have chilled, they can be stored and transported in an airtight container for up to a week. Put parchment paper between layers to prevent sticking.

HOMEMADE GRANOLA BARS

Making your own granola bars may seem like overkill, something you only do if you also live on a homestead and wear bonnets and raise chickens and make your own butter. All of which, actually, are activities that I'm totally here for, so, maybe that explains something. Anyway, if you ever look at your grocery receipts and notice just how much money you spend on organic granola bars for your three-year-old who houses them like they are the base of the food pyramid, suddenly making your own granola bars seems like a reasonable and frugal activity. Plus they taste better than the store-bought kind, and they pack quite well. Throw a container in your backpack to prevent mid-hike meltdowns.

Ingredients

1¼ cups (125 g) rolled oats

⅓ cup (46 g) whole wheat flour (replace with ground flaxseed for a gluten-free bar)

3 tablespoons (27 g) cornmeal

1 cup (175 g) finely chopped pitted dates

1 teaspoon salt

½ teaspoon ground cinnamon

⅓ cup (115 g) honey

¼ cup (59 ml) olive oil

¼ cup (65 g) creamy peanut butter

½ teaspoon lemon zest

Make It

1. Heat your oven to 350°F (180°C, or gas mark 4). Line an 8" x 8" (20 x 20 cm) baking pan with parchment paper. (Tinfoil will also work. With most baking projects I don't use parchment paper, but for these I really recommend lining your baking pan if you want the bars to come out without breaking apart.)

2. In one bowl, combine the oats, whole wheat flour, cornmeal, dates, salt, and cinnamon. In a separate bowl, whisk together the honey, olive oil, peanut butter, and lemon zest. Scrape the wet ingredients into the bowl of the dry ingredients and stir well until everything is completely coated.

3. Dump the mixture into the prepared pan and pat it into an even layer with your fingers (there's enough olive oil that it won't stick to your fingers). Bake for 20–25 minutes or until well browned around the edges but still soft in the center. Cool the bars to room temperature, then use a sharp knife to cut into ten pieces, about 4" x 1½" (10 x 4 cm). Stack the bars in a sealed, airtight container with parchment paper between the layers and allow them to chill in the fridge for at least another 30 minutes to fully set them. Store and transport in the airtight container.

> **NOTE:** Can't do nuts? Tahini or sun butter will also work well in these granola bars.

KAITLIN'S TIPS FOR
GLUTEN-FREE LUNCHES AND SNACKING

I have celiac disease, and my whole family generally eats gluten free to avoid cross contamination and making me sick—especially while camping, as it can be hard to find a spot for a really good handwashing after little hands have enjoyed gluten snacks. Our favorite and easy gluten-free camping snacks include trail mixes of all kinds, gluten-free granola bars, and salty snacks, especially rice crackers and gluten-free pretzels.

Almost every lunch on trail as a child with my family, as a canoe guide, or now with my own children has been the same: a bread item, summer sausage, cheese, peanut butter and jelly, and trail mix. These days, I add a piece of fruit to be fancy. All of these items can be found in gluten-free versions. Keep in mind that your lunch is likely going to be eaten cold on the go, so plan accordingly. I personally find gluten-free bagels to be inedible unless they are toasted, so I try to stay away from them unless I know I'll be by a fire for lunch. Gluten-free crackers are a great choice if you are car camping. For sturdier sandwiches, bring a loaf of your favorite gluten-free bread or a package of gluten-free Wasa crackers. Crackers easily get crushed and bread loaves easily smushed when camping, so make sure to have a hard-sided container of some kind for packing your lunch items. There's nothing worse than pulling out your box of crackers on day four to find that they are crushed into hundreds of impossible-to-eat-with-peanut-butter tiny pieces.

CHOOSE YOUR OWN ADVENTURE TRAIL MIX

There's nothing wrong with "good old raisins and peanuts" (GORP), the most classic trail mix. In fact, I used to practically live off it on camping trips. Or to be more accurate, I lived off the M&Ms I meticulously picked out of it. But, when it comes down to it, trail mix is really just a mix of things you like to snack on, all thrown together. So, why not choose your own adventure? Choose a nut (if you can have nuts), a dried fruit or two, a treat, and a crunchy element and build the trail mix of your dreams. Here are some options to get you started.

NUTTY OPTION

Peanuts

Toasted almonds

Walnuts

Toasted hazelnuts

Pepitas

FRUITY OPTION

Dried cherries

Dried mango bits and golden raisins

Dried cranberries

Banana chips

Chopped dried figs

Dried apricots

SWEET OPTION

Chocolate chips

M&Ms

White chocolate chips

Yogurt-covered raisins

Milk chocolate chips or disks

Chopped crystalized ginger

CRUNCHY OPTION

Pretzels

Toasted coconut flakes

Popcorn

Toasted oat O's cereal (such as Cheerios)

Rye pretzels

Chex cereal

KIND OF FANCY GOLDFISH SNACK MIX

Yes, this is a snack mix we serve at our bar at Vikre. But, my husband often grabs some to snack on, and it winds up in his car, and our kids spot it and love it. So, what can I say? Kid friendly? Fiery crunchy wasabi peas, savory sesame sticks, and bits of nori take cheesy goldfish in an unexpectedly tasty direction.

Ingredients

4 cups (804 g) cheesy Goldfish crackers (you could use other cheese crackers, but then you wouldn't get to think about how funny it is to have fish and seaweed together in your snack mix)

1 cup (120 g) sesame sticks

1 cup (91 g) wasabi peas

1 sheet nori, cut into short, thin strips, kind of like seaweed confetti

Make It

Stir all of the ingredients together and transfer them into a tightly sealed container! That's it!

LUNCHES TO ENJOY AT YOUR CAMPSITE

CHICKPEA SALAD WITH PITA

It's the flavors of a falafel wrap with tahini sauce turned into a salad! Is this mostly inspired by the falafel sandwiches at Falafel Palace where, when we were in our 20s, my friends and I would go at 2:30 in the morning for a snack after dancing all night? Yes, yes it is. Don't tell my kids.

Ingredients

1 large garnet yam, peeled and cut into 1-inch (2.5 cm) cubes

Olive oil

Salt

1 15-ounce (425 g) can chickpeas, drained and rinsed

2 garlic cloves, peeled

1 tablespoon (40 g) chopped red onion

1 tablespoon (15 g) tahini

1 teaspoon ground cumin

¼ cup (60 ml) fresh lemon juice

½ cup (30 g) chopped fresh parsley

FOR SERVING

Cucumber slices

Cherry tomatoes, halved

Pitas or another soft flatbread

Make It

AT HOME

1. Heat your oven to 425°F (220°C, or gas mark 7). Toss the cubed yam with about 1 tablespoon (15 ml) of olive oil and sprinkle it with salt. Spread on a baking sheet and roast, stirring occasionally until cooked through and browned on the outside, about 40 minutes.

2. In a frying pan over medium heat, add about 1 tablespoon (15 ml) of olive oil and heat until shimmering. Add the chickpeas and the whole garlic cloves. Cook, stirring, until the garlic is golden on the outside and the chickpeas are warmed, about 3–4 minutes. Remove from heat.

3. Finely chop the two sautéed garlic cloves. In a large bowl, whisk together the garlic, red onion, tahini, cumin, 1 tablespoon (15 ml) of olive oil, lemon juice, and a generous pinch of salt (I find tahini to be very bitter without a good hit of salt). Whisk a spoonful of water into the dressing if you need to increase its creaminess and make it thinner. Add the cooked yam, chickpeas, and parsley and toss to coat everything with the dressing. Taste and add more salt, if desired. Allow to cool to room temperature, then transfer to an airtight container.

IN CAMP

Serve the chickpea salad scooped into pita breads along with slices of cucumber and cherry tomato halves. I always let my kids do the scooping and adding of cucumbers and tomatoes themselves. They use an unreasonable number of cucumber slices and not very many chickpeas, but there are worse problems to have.

BLACK BEAN AND AVOCADO QUESADILLA

Over the past couple of years, quesadillas have become one of our go-to kid lunches, and none of us are sad about it. Gooey cheese in golden tortillas, need I say more? We make plain cheese quesadillas a *lot*. But, my older son also requests black bean and avocado quesadillas, and I feel like if your kid asks for beans, get them their beans!

Ingredients

4 9-inch (23 cm) flour tortillas

2 cups (230 g) shredded Oaxacan cheese (or Monterey Jack)

1 14-ounce (396 g) can of black beans, drained

1 ripe avocado, peel removed and cut into slices

Make It

1. Heat a skillet over medium heat and place a tortilla in the skillet. Sprinkle about ½ cup (58 g) cheese all over it. Then on one half of the tortilla, add some black beans and one fourth of the avocado slices.

2. Cover and cook for a couple minutes until the cheese melts and the tortilla has browned on the underside. Remove the pan lid and fold the half with just cheese over the half with the other toppings. Transfer the quesadilla to a plate and repeat to make the remaining quesadillas. Slice the quesadillas into wedges before eating.

VEGGIE FRIED RICE

It's hard to say for certain what the highest calling may be for leftover rice, but fried rice is definitely in the running. Who can resist a lunch of chewy rice, bronzed and soaked with soy and sesame, spiked with fragrant scallions and ginger, all ready in a matter of minutes? Plus, I have to award it bonus points because you can hide vegetables in it. When I have my druthers, I also pile my bowl of fried rice with kimchi as a funky, spicy crown, but I serve it on the side so everyone can choose their level of funk.

Ingredients

3 tablespoons (45 ml) oil or butter

3 large garlic cloves, thinly sliced

2 tablespoons (12 g) minced ginger

1 bunch of scallions, tips removed, thinly sliced

4 cups (880 g) leftover cooked rice

¼ cup (60 ml) soy sauce

1 tablespoon (15 ml) sesame oil

1–2 cups (71–142 g) chopped leftover vegetables of any variety (carrots, peas, greens, broccoli, cauliflower, they all work well here)

4 eggs, lightly beaten

Kimchi for serving (optional)

Make It

1. Heat a large skillet over high heat, add the butter or oil, and allow them to get hot but not smoking. Stir in the garlic and let it sizzle for a minute, then add the ginger and scallions and turn the heat down to medium. Cook until the scallions have started to soften, about 1–2 minutes.

2. Stir in the rice, soy sauce, sesame oil, and vegetables. Allow to cook for 3–5 minutes, stirring just once or twice until the rice is quite hot and getting crusty and sticking to the pan in a couple places. Pour the eggs onto the rice and cook, stirring well, for another couple minutes until the egg is cooked through and distributed throughout.

3. Serve the fried rice with kimchi and additional sesame oil for drizzling, if desired.

QUINOA, CORN, AND BACON SALAD

There are some ingredients that make my kids squeal with delight: "Corn!" and "Bacon!" are two of them. So, I sometimes add them to other ingredients as a way to get my kids to try it. Such was the genesis of this grain salad. The quinoa makes it extra filling as well as gluten free. But, if you were to make it with pasta instead, thus creating a corn, bacon, and pasta salad, I can guarantee it would go alright. It might even induce the triple squeal.

Ingredients

¾ cup (129 g) quinoa, rinsed

1½ cups (355 ml) water

4 ears of corn

5 ounces (140 g) bacon, cut into small pieces

¼ cup (59 g) olive oil, divided

1 red onion, thinly sliced

Salt

2 teaspoons (9 g) sugar

¼ cup (60 ml) balsamic vinegar, divided

Make It

1. Combine the quinoa and water in a pot. Bring to a boil, then reduce heat to a simmer, cover, and simmer until the water is absorbed and the quinoa is tender, about 15 minutes. Set aside.

2. Remove the kernels from the ears of corn. Set aside.

3. In a large skillet, fry the bacon pieces over medium-high heat until they are brown and crispy, around 5–7 minutes. Using a slotted spoon, transfer the bacon bits to a plate lined with a paper towel.

4. Pour off all but 1 tablespoon (15 ml) of bacon fat from the skillet, add 1 tablespoon (15 ml) of olive oil, and stir in the onion plus a sprinkling of salt. Cook the onion over medium-high heat until it starts to soften, about 2–3 minutes. Then turn the heat down to medium-low, stir in the sugar and 2 tablespoons of vinegar, and cook until soft and lumpy, about 20 minutes.

5. Stir in the corn kernels and cook until the kernels have barely cooked, about 5 minutes. Remove from the heat.

6. Whisk together the remaining oil and balsamic vinegar. Toss this dressing with the cooked quinoa, stir in the corn mixture, then season with salt to taste. When the salad has cooled to room temperature, transfer it into a well-sealed container and refrigerate. Pack the container of salad in your cooler to bring to camp. This makes a great lunch salad or dinner side dish, and you can eat it cold or quickly warmed up in a hot pan.

"MEATBALL" AND VEGETABLE SOUP

This is our family's signature soup. I made this soup for dinner just the other night, and my three-year-old turned to me, his face smeared with broth and carrots, and he said (and this is a real quote, not a quote from a paid three-year-old actor!), "Thank you for making this delicious soup with everything I like." And for a brief and glorious moment I felt like I was really, really good at parenting. Then he turned to his older brother and called him a poopy face and the golden moment faded. But the point holds, and the point is that this is a good soup.

Ingredients

1 tablespoon (15 ml) olive oil

2 shallots, finely chopped

4 small-medium red potatoes, cut into 1½-inch (4 cm) cubes

3 medium carrots, cut into 1-inch (2.5 cm) cubes

2 cups (280 g) cubed butternut squash

1 bunch of lacinato kale, washed, tough stem ends removed, and cut into 1-inch (2.5 cm) ribbons

4 cups (946 ml) water plus 4 teaspoons (16.8 g) Better Than Bouillon vegetable bouillon (or 4 cups [946 ml] really good broth)

1 pound (455 g) mild Italian sausage

1 teaspoon white wine vinegar

Salt to taste

Make It

1. In a large pot, heat the olive oil over medium-high heat. Add the shallot and cook until softened, about 2–3 minutes. Stir in the potatoes, carrots, and squash and cook for a couple of minutes. Stir in the kale and cook for 1–2 minutes or until it has begun to wilt.

2. Stir in the water and Better Than Bouillon. (Just as a side note, I've become a massive convert to Better Than Bouillon in the last couple of years. The flavor is just fantastic, and I find it easier to keep a jar of that around than broth. But if you have really good broth or stock, go ahead and use that.) Bring to a boil, stirring, then turn down to a simmer.

3. Simmer the soup for about 20 minutes. Then add the Italian sausage in little 1½-inch (4 cm) meatballs. If you are using sausage in casings, just squeeze it out of the casings in 1½-inch (4 cm) pieces, breaking them off directly into the soup. If you have bulk sausage, gently roll the sausage into 1½-inch (4 cm) balls, taking care not to compress them too much as you roll, then drop them into the soup.

4. Simmer the soup until the vegetables are soft, another 10–15 minutes. Then stir in the vinegar. Add more salt to taste, if desired. If making ahead, allow the soup to cool to room temperature before transferring to a leak-proof container to freeze. Make sure you leave an inch (2.5 cm) of headspace in the container you use as the soup will expand as it freezes.

5. In camp, make sure the soup has thawed, then gently reheat it in a pot over medium heat.

TIP: You can make a simple soup at your campsite to be sure. But try this instead: Make soup ahead of time, transfer it to a tightly sealed container, and freeze it. Then the soup does double duty as an ice pack in your cooler before it becomes an extra quick lunch or dinner when you need it!

HEARTY TOMATO SOUP

The funny thing about soup in our family is my kids love it, and it's my husband who whines when I put a pot on the table. But I invariably win him over with hearty, flavorful soups. We are all delighted with a tomato soup that is creamy but full of texture and punctuated with aromatic fennel. Just add grilled cheese!

Ingredients

2 tablespoons (28 g) butter

1 large fennel bulb, stems removed, bottom trimmed off, cored, and chopped into 1-inch (2.5 cm) pieces

1 yellow onion, diced

2 carrots, cut into 1-inch (2.5 cm) pieces

2 celery stalks, diced

½ cup (120 ml) white wine (optional but lovely!)

2 14.5-ounce (800 g) cans crushed tomatoes

1 teaspoon sugar

2 cups (470 ml) water plus 2 teaspoons (8.4 g) Better Than Bouillon (or 2 cups [470 ml] good broth

2 cups (470 ml) heavy cream

Salt to taste

Make It

1. In a large pot over medium-high heat, heat the butter until it foams, then stir in the fennel and onion. Cook until the onion softens slightly, about 2 minutes, then stir in the carrots and celery. Turn the heat to medium, cover, and let the vegetables cook (lift the lid and stir occasionally) until they have softened quite a bit, about 10 minutes. If they start to brown too much, lower the heat.

2. Uncover, pour in the wine, and cook for a couple of minutes, then add the tomatoes, sugar, and broth or water plus bouillon. Bring to a simmer, then turn down the heat and cook over medium-low heat for about 30 minutes until all the vegetables are quite tender, crushing up the tomatoes with a wooden spoon as they cook.

3. Stir in the heavy cream and add salt to taste.

4. If making ahead, allow the soup to cool to room temperature before transferring to a leak-proof container to freeze. Make sure you leave an inch (2.5 cm) of headspace in the jar or other container you use as the soup will expand as it freezes. If you have chosen to use a glass canning jar, be careful not to expose it to fast temperature changes as the thermal shock can cause cracking.

5. In camp, make sure the soup has thawed fully, then gently reheat it in a pot over medium heat. Serve on its own or with grilled cheese sandwiches.

NORWEGIAN STICK BREAD (*PINNEBRØD*) WITH GARLIC BUTTER

The other day, I was texting back and forth with my sister-in-law, Eline, in Norway about favorite *pinnebrød* recipes. It's a classic Norwegian camping and hiking food—quick bread dough made at home, then twisted around a stick in camp and baked over an open fire. She laughed (well, emoji-laughed) and said, "They never really taste that good, do they? But it is so fun to burn dough on a stick it does not matter." A few moments later she wondered about adding extra flavors, like something sweet or maybe garlic butter. The moment I saw the words "garlic butter," my mouth started watering, and I knew she was onto something. The garlic butter makes these soft twirls of dough taste like garlic bread sticks with a hint of campfire char.

The real trick to *pinnebrød* is to take it easy, kind of like with marshmallows. Hold them over a burned-down portion of the fire, spin them as needed, and be patient because they take around 10 minutes to cook. This way, the dough will bake through without burning on the outside. When baked properly, they are quite good, even without the garlic butter. Of course, even if you do burn the outside, as Eline pointed out, it doesn't really matter! "The process is more of a ritual and matters more than the taste."

Ingredients

FOR THE BREAD DOUGH

3⅓ cups (417 g) flour

1 teaspoon salt

1 tablespoon (13 g) sugar

1 tablespoon (14 g) baking powder

½ cup plus 2 tablespoons oil (150 ml) (I just use olive oil, as I do for most things that call for oil)

1¼ cups (295 ml) water

FOR THE GARLIC BUTTER

½ cup (112 g) butter

4 garlic cloves, minced

Make It

AT HOME

1. Combine all the dry ingredients for the bread in a large bowl and make a well in the center.

2. In another container, whisk together the oil and water to emulsify them, then drizzle this into the well in the dry ingredients. Mix everything together with a wooden spoon until a shaggy ball forms.

3. Get in there with your hands and knead the dough 8–10 times to pick up any flour that wasn't incorporated, bringing it together into a smooth dough ball.

4. Coat the dough ball with some additional oil, then transfer it to a zip-top bag or sealed container to transport.

IN CAMP

1. In a small pot, heat the butter until it is melted. Stir in the minced garlic and cook for a minute until it has softened. (I do this because I don't really like raw garlic, but I love cooked garlic. If you're into raw garlic in your garlic butter, then just melt the butter and stir in the garlic off the heat.)

2. Break off pieces of dough that are about the size of a walnut, roll them into thin ropes, and twist them around cooking sticks (use sturdy, green tree branches like the kind you would use for hot dogs. Make sure they are sturdy enough to hold a breadstick. I haven't tried using metal marshmallow/hot dog roasting sticks, but I bet it could

work!). Brush the outside of the bread twist with a bit of garlic butter, then cook over fire embers, turning often until the bread is browned on the outside and cooked through to the middle. Repeat to make as many bread twists as you want.

3. Brush with more garlic butter and eat warm. Leftover dough can be cooked as flatbread in a skillet using the method found in the dahl with flatbread recipe on page 137.

CHAPTER FOUR

DINNER

◆

There's something about camping that induces voraciousness. No matter how hearty the other meals during the day have been, when suppertime rolls around, tummies are grumbling. This means it's time to whip up a meal that is delicious and satisfying but quick enough to circumvent any hunger-induced grumpiness—especially because I'm not really one to allow much snacking while we wait for dinner, except for cheese trays, which are exempt from the snacking category. (This couuuuuld be related to how voracious we are at dinner, but correlation is not causation, you know!) For camping, I love a good one-pot meal where all (or at least most) of the elements are combined into a single, glorious mélange. It minimizes dishes, burner use, and issues with timing different parts of a meal. At home if I try to serve a one-pot meal, my kids look at me quizzically and ask, "Where are the other parts of dinner?" But when we're camping, no questions asked!

Most of the time, I'm a tornado in the kitchen. I chop as I go, clean as I go, and I don't measure or time anything. It's not a good cooking technique, per se, but it's gotten me this far. When we're camping, it's a different story. I definitely counsel you to use good mise en place, that is to say, measure and chop all your ingredients in advance before you start any actual cooking. Campfires and camp stoves are basically living—and somewhat temperamental—creatures with their own whims and opinions about how hot they are going to be at any given moment. You have to base your cooking on visual cues more than you might with a more predictable heat source, so you want all your ingredients ready to rumble in order to avoid scrambling.

THE BEST CAMP MACARONI AND CHEESE

If there is one thing we can always agree on when we are camping it's . . . s'mores. But pasta takes a close second place. I don't know about you, but for me, parenting is one drawn-out attempt to get my kids to eat something that isn't a carb + cheese. I parade before them with all sorts of delicious vegetables and spices, stews, and sautés. What they really want is: mac and cheese, grilled cheese, quesadillas, and pizza. Sometimes, I just have to give it to them. This is a very simple one-pot macaroni and cheese that is barely more effort than making the kind from a box. The only bit that could be considered an effort is whisking the milk into the flour, but I really think you are up for it. And if not, well, boxed mac and cheese is still delicious in its own way.

Ingredients

Water

8 ounces (225 g) short, twirly pasta, such as elbow noodles, fusilli, or small shells

2 tablespoons (28 g) butter

1 tablespoon (8 g) flour

¾ cup (175 ml) whole milk

½ cup (50 g) grated Parmesan

½ cup (60 g) grated mild cheddar cheese

Salt and pepper

ADD-INS: There are all sorts of delicious things you can stir into macaroni and cheese. Our favorites are chopped fresh tomato, salted avocado chunks, peas, or hot dog slices (see page 118 for more on my feelings about hot dogs).

Make It

1. On your camp stove, bring a large pot of water to a boil. Once boiling, salt the water well and add the pasta. Cook until the pasta is al dente, then drain the pasta and set it aside.

2. Put the pot back on the stove over medium heat and add the butter. Cook the butter until it is foaming, then stir in the flour to make a paste. Cook the flour for half a minute, then begin to stir in the milk a splash at a time, stirring well, and working quickly to make sure that no lumps form. Once all the milk is stirred in, bring to a simmer and simmer for 1 minute, stirring constantly.

3. Stir in the cooked pasta and the cheeses, and cook for 1 more minute, stirring all the while to coat the pasta well. Season with salt and pepper to taste and serve.

ORZO WITH KALE, TOMATO, AND FETA

It's rather like risotto, but so much less stirring! The tomato, kale, and fennel collaborate like a well-managed team to build a flavorful and toothsome vegetarian dish, the eating of which makes me feel a bit like a happy peasant in Italy—which is a feeling I'll take any day. Hot tip: Go ahead and eat the lemon slices! The cooking makes them absolutely scrumptious.

Ingredients

3 tablespoons (45 ml) olive oil

1⅓ cups (280 g) orzo

2 teaspoons fennel seeds

3 cloves garlic, minced

½ lemon, cut into thin slices, seeds removed

1 bunch lacinto kale, stems removed, finely chopped

1 14.5-ounce (400 g) can crushed tomatoes

2 cubes vegetable bouillon (or 2 teaspoons Better than Bouillon)

2 ¾ cups (650 ml) water

Salt and pepper

½ cup (75 g) crumbled feta cheese

Fresh mint (optional)

Make It

1. Heat 2 tablespoons (30 ml) olive oil in a large skillet over high heat. When the oil is shimmering, stir in the orzo and cook for about 3 minutes, stirring until the orzo starts to turn golden brown.

2. Stir in the remaining olive oil, the fennel seeds, garlic, and lemon slices and fry for 1–2 minutes until the garlic has softened. Stir in the kale and cook just long enough for the kale to start to wilt, then add the tomatoes, bouillon, water, and 1 teaspoon salt and bring to a boil, stirring constantly.

3. Decrease the heat to medium-low and cover. Simmer for about 15 minutes, stirring every now and then to make sure the orzo doesn't get stuck to the bottom of the pan. Remove the cover and cook for 2–3 more minutes until the pasta and sauce has a loose porridge-like consistency. Sprinkle with feta, and adjust the salt and pepper to taste, then serve. This is good with fresh mint sprinkled over it, if you brought any for mojitos.

GLUTEN-FREE PASTA
TIPS AND PREFERENCES
from Kaitlin

Eating gluten free, one of the most important things to figure out was what to do about pasta! Gluten-free pasta generally does not hold up well in one-pot pastas where the pasta is cooked directly in the sauce. So, opt for a two-pot method, cooking the sauce in one pot and your pasta in another, then mixing at the end when everything is cooked. Our favorite gluten-free pastas are the varieties that are brown-rice based.

SKILLET "LASAGNA"

Lasagna is the Coziest. With a capital C. It's also a pain in the butt to make, even under the best of circumstances. This simple skillet version subverts all of lasagna's usual pain points—all the prep bowls, all the layering, all the long bake times—by plopping everything together. And you know what? It's almost just as good. Actually, maybe it's better because you'll be making it and eating it instead of trying to remember whether you need a layer of ricotta or sauce next!

I will say, while overall this might be the easiest lasagna you ever do encounter, breaking lasagna noodles into small bits is kind of a job. It's a good task for a seven-year-old boy with an affinity for breaking things. Or, if you aren't committed to lasagna made with lasagna noodles, you could instead use a smaller type of noodle, such as penne or conchiglie.

Ingredients

1 tablespoon (15 ml) olive oil

1 pound (455 g) bulk mild Italian sausage

4 cloves garlic, finely chopped

1 teaspoon dried oregano

1 24-ounce (730 g) jar tomato sauce

2 bay leaves

1 teaspoon salt

12 ounces (340 g) lasagna noodles (the regular kind, not the no-cook kind), broken into 1-inch-wide (2.5 cm) pieces

1½ cups (355 ml) water

1 cup (250 g) whole-milk ricotta

⅓ cup (27 g) shredded Parmesan

8 ounces (225 g) fresh mozzarella, torn into 1-inch (2.5 cm) chunks

Fresh basil for serving (optional)

Make It

1. In a 12-inch (30 cm) cast-iron skillet, heat the olive oil over medium-high heat on your camp stove until it is shimmering. Then stir in the sausage and cook, breaking apart the sausage into small pieces until it browns, about 5 minutes. Stir in the garlic and oregano and cook for about 1 more minute. Add the tomato sauce and the bay leaves and cook for 2 minutes, stirring occasionally.

2. Add the salt, noodle pieces, and water and stir well (or, at least, as well as you can without spilling over the sides of the skillet). Bring to a boil, then turn the heat down to medium-low to keep the pan at a peppy simmer. Cover your pan and cook for 15 minutes, removing the cover and stirring the noodles around every so often to keep them from sticking too much and to make sure they are all getting coated with sauce—any noodles that stay too stuck together may not cook through.

3. In the meantime, stir the Parmesan cheese into the ricotta in a small bowl. After the pasta has cooked for 15 minutes, uncover, fish out the bay leaves, and then dollop the ricotta mixture throughout the pasta. Sprinkle the mozzarella chunks over the top, cover, and cook for 5 more minutes. Remove from the heat and sprinkle with torn basil, if you have it. Allow to cool for 5 minutes before serving.

PASTA WITH DILLY YOGURT AND LAMB

This is one of our family's absolute smash-hit, oft-requested, always-enjoyed dinners, in any season. It is a streamlined version of a variation on a variation of a Middle Eastern lamb dumpling dish. So, I can't say it has that much in common with the original dish any longer, but it still has the important flavor combination of lamb, dill, yogurt, and lemon that we can never get enough of. It's not a meal that makes you immediately think, "Camp food!" when you see it. But, the very first time I ever made it was a summer evening when our power had gone out at home from a storm. We had reached the part of the day when our whole family is a mix of weepy and grumpy from hunger (You feel me, right?!), and my dinner plan had just been pulled, rug-like, out from under me because we have an electric stove. After shedding just a couple extra tears of annoyance, we pulled out the camping stove, this marvelous supper came together in minutes, and the evening was saved.

Ingredients

Water

1 pound (455 g) ground lamb

1 tablespoon (7 g) ground cumin

Salt

2 cloves garlic, finely chopped

½ cup (75 g) raisins

8 ounces (225 g) small sturdy pasta, such as orecchiette, small shells, farfalle, or strozzapretti

1½ cups (345 g) whole-milk yogurt

2 eggs

1 large bunch fresh dill, very finely chopped

1 lemon, sliced into wedges

Make It

1. On one burner of your camp stove, start heating a pot of water to a boil. On the other burner, heat a skillet over medium-high heat and add the ground lamb.

2. Smash the lamb down with a spatula or spoon and sprinkle the cumin, 1 teaspoon of salt, and the chopped garlic over it. Allow the lamb to brown without stirring it, about 3–4 minutes, then flip the lamb over and break it apart with your spatula. Stir in the raisins and cook them along with the meat until the meat is fully cooked, another couple of minutes. Set aside.

3. When the water comes to a boil, salt the water well and add the pasta. Cook until the pasta is al dente, then drain the pasta. Add the hot pasta back into the pot along with the yogurt and the eggs and cook for 1–2 minutes on low heat, stirring well to mix everything together. Remove from the heat, stir in the chopped dill, and add more salt to taste.

4. To serve, divide the pasta among plates, sprinkle with the lamb and raisin mixture, and allow everyone to squeeze the lemon wedges over, to taste. (The lemon really makes the dish shine.)

STOVETOP TUNA NOODLE "CASSEROLE"

I grew up mostly in Minnesota, but as I mentioned earlier, my mom is from Norway, so our standard dinner rotation was always a little different from our neighbors'. I have fond, funny memories of my mom trying to wrap her brain around the "hotdish" and why you would make one, combined with her deep sense of pride whenever she did make a casserole. Tuna noodle casserole was always my favorite, and it's a dish my husband requests whenever I can't think of what to make for dinner. Our kids, on the other hand, don't like it at all, but that's their tough luck. All the other kids we know do! This version is made entirely on the stovetop so you can make it in a single pot on your camp stove. At home, I make a béchamel sauce as for mac and cheese, but for camping, I rather like to throw it back and use the original cream of mushroom soup.

Ingredients

Water

8 ounces (225 g) pasta with pretty short noodles, such as fusilli, conchiglie, or small shells

1 tablespoon (14 g) butter or olive oil

1 small yellow onion, diced

1 stalk celery, diced

1 10.5-ounce (295 g) can cream of mushroom soup

1 15-ounce (483 g) can peas, drained, or 2 cups (260 g) frozen peas, defrosted

1 cup (80 g) shredded Parmesan

2 5-ounce (280 g) cans chunk light tuna, drained, or 2 packets of chunk light tuna

Salt and pepper

Make It

1. Fill a large pot with water and bring to a boil over high heat on your camp stove. When the water has come to a rolling boil, add 1 tablespoon (18 g) salt and your pasta. Cook according to the directions on the pasta package until the pasta is al dente. Using a heat-resistant cup or ladle, reserve 1½ cups (355 ml) of the pasta water and set it aside. Drain the pasta and set it to the side.

2. Return the pot to your camp stove, add butter or oil, and turn the heat down to medium. Stir in the onion and celery and cook, stirring until the onion is translucent, about 2 minutes. Stir in the cream of mushroom soup, reserved pasta water, and peas, cooking until the mixture starts simmering.

3. Add the cooked noodles, Parmesan, and canned tuna, stirring until the noodles are coated and the Parmesan has melted into the sauce. Season with salt and pepper to taste before serving.

CAMP BEEF STROGANOFF

I couldn't sleep. And it wasn't because I was wedged onto our friends' less than comfortable couch, though I'll admit that wasn't helping much. It was because of the smell of stroganoff that thickly permeated the air. Our friends Hillary and Erik were getting ready to go on a long hiking trip, and they were preparing all of their own food. This is admirable, but it meant their dehydrator was running 24/7, and their house smelled 24/7. During our visit, it was stroganoff. Dehydrated beef stroganoff is a classic, *classic* camping meal. But I can't say I've ever been a fan. When it comes to dehydrated meals, I am a cheesy rice gal all the way. Anyway, while dehydrated stroganoff might cut it for tough hiking, when you're car camping, there is another way. And that way is a rich plate of steak and sour cream goodness. I think this is a good second night in camp meal. You're settled enough to make a dinner that's a little more involved, and the steak will have defrosted by then.

Ingredients

2 tablespoons (30 ml) Worcestershire sauce, divided

1 tablespoon (15 ml) balsamic vinegar

1 pound (455 g) strip steak, hangar steak, or another good cut of steak for stir-fry, cut across the grain into 2-inch (5 cm) pieces

2 tablespoons (28 g) butter, divided

1 small yellow onion, finely chopped

2 garlic cloves, minced

8 ounces (225 g) button or cremini mushrooms, quartered

1 teaspoon dried thyme

¼ cup (59 ml) red wine (optional but recommended)

2 cups (473 ml) water (plus more as needed)

1 bouillon cube (or 1 teaspoon Better than Bouillon)

8 ounces (225 g) egg noodles

½ cup (115 g) sour cream

Salt

Make It

AT HOME

Combine 1 tablespoon (15 ml) Worcestershire sauce and the balsamic vinegar in a heavy-duty zip top bag, add the steak, and squeeze the marinade around onto the surface of the steak. Seal well and freeze. Before leaving, pack the bag into your cooler.

IN CAMP

1. Heat a large, deep skillet over medium-high heat and add 1 tablespoon (14 g) butter. Allow the butter to melt and foam, then remove the steak from the marinade and place it in the pan. Cook the steak pieces until they are browned and cooked through. How long this takes will depend on the steak, but it's usually around 3–5 minutes. Transfer the steak to a plate.

2. Add the remaining butter to the skillet and once melted, add the onion and garlic. Cook, stirring for 3 minutes, then add the mushrooms and season with a bit of salt. Cook the mushrooms and onion until the mushrooms are softened, about 5–8 more minutes.

continued

3. Stir in the thyme, red wine if using, water, and bouillon. Add the egg noodles and bring to a boil, stirring to coat the noodles with the sauce. Cover and cook, uncovering to stir occasionally, until the noodles are soft. This will depend on the brand of noodles you are using, usually in the realm of 5 minutes or up to 10 minutes for thicker noodles. As the noodles cook, add more water if the pan seems to be getting too dry.

4. When the noodles are cooked through, remove the pan from the heat and stir in the sour cream a little bit at a time. Stir in the steak slices. Adjust the salt to taste and serve. I like to serve this with steamed broccoli as a side. It just works.

NOTES FROM KAITLIN, A WILDERNESS GUIDE

As a young twenty-something canoe guide, I remember cooking premixed, dehydrated beef stroganoff in the rain over a smoky fire. It inevitably ended up too gummy or too watery or the noodles were somehow undercooked even though the stroganoff mix burned to the bottom of the pan. It certainly never ended up being tasty. Thankfully for all of us, Emily's beef stroganoff is not the canoe camp variety, and I promise it will be delicious.

OH THE THINGS YOU CAN DO WITH HOT DOGS

True confession: Our family eats a lot of hot dogs. Year-round, for any occasion, not just camping. It would be embarrassing, except that we love them so much, I've decided I just have to accept it. (And we are lucky enough to have friends who sustainably and humanely raise pastured pork and make small batch hot dogs, which is what we buy, so that helps too.) As with many things, I'm quite sure our love of hot dogs is tied to our summers in Norway where *pølse med lompe*—hot dogs with a soft, tortilla-like potato flatbread related to Norwegian potato lefse—was a staple. That said, when I think of camping food, hot dogs are my go-to, and it took some real effort not to make this whole book into *The Great Book of Eating Hot Dogs*. But now, on this page, it's the hot dog's time to shine!

A plain hot dog with ketchup or mustard is never a wrong answer, but here are just a few of the many other fun ways you can serve hot dogs.

- **BÁNH MI DOG:** Add pickled vegetables (preferably carrot, cucumber, and daikon radish), mayo, and sriracha to your hot dog and bun. Sprinkle with jalapeño slices and cilantro to really complete the bánh mi effect.

- **HOT DOG TACOS:** Slice your cooked hot dogs into half-inch (1 cm) slices and serve them in flour tortillas with shredded cabbage, sour cream, salsa, and lime. Or, serve your hot dog on a tortilla with guac and black beans.

- **HOT DOGS AL PASTOR:** Grill some pineapple and red onion slices alongside your hot dogs. Then serve your hot dog topped with the grilled pineapple and onion, plus a squeeze of lime and a sprinkle of cilantro.

- **HOT DOG CARBONARA:** Cook a pot of spaghetti noodles and reserve about one cup of the pasta water before draining the noodles. Toss the hot pasta with a couple of whisked eggs, plenty of Parmesan cheese, and enough pasta water to make the egg and cheese into a thick sauce, then fold in cooked hot dog slices before serving.

- **HOT DOG SALAD:** Sprinkle cooked hot dog chopped into small bits over a wedge salad or Caesar salad, like hot dog croutons!

- **BREAKFAST DOG:** Dice your hot dogs and fry them in a skillet until lightly browned. Serve with fried eggs and hash browns.

- **THE NORWEGIAN DOG (AKA LEFSE DOG):** This is the best way to eat a hot dog, in my humble opinion. It's so good. Cook your hot dogs and serve each rolled in a piece of Norwegian potato lefse. Top with ketchup and deep-fried crispy onions.

CAMPFIRE NACHOS

Whether you make a dinner of nachos (been there) or want to make some for lunch or a predinner snack, this is less a recipe per se and more me letting you know: You can make nachos in a foil pack over a grill! Or on a grate over your campfire!

Ingredients

MUST HAVE

Aluminum foil

1 8-ounce (225 g) bag corn chips (about 6 or 7 cups [156 or 182 g] of chips)

2½ cups (283 g) shredded cheese, preferably a mix of mild cheddar and Jack cheese, but just one or the other works as well

Sour cream and salsa for serving

NICE TO HAVE

About 1 cup (225 g) precooked shredded pork or chicken

1 cup (256 g) canned black beans, drained and rinsed

1 large tomato, diced

Jalapeño slices

Canned black olives

Pickled red onions (page 83)

Make It

1. Lay out two sheets of aluminum foil that are each about 12" x 24" (30 x 60 cm). On each sheet, lay down a cup of chips in a single layer, then sprinkle one quarter of the cheese over the top. If you are using any of the other nice-to-have things, sprinkle some on the layer as well. Add another layer of chips to each foil pack, sprinkle with the remainder of cheese (and other toppings), then top with the remainder of the chips. Having chips on both the top and bottom helps prevent some of the cheese from getting stuck to the foil, although collateral cheese loss is just kind of part of the life of nachos.

2. Fold the foil packets over and roll the edges tightly together to seal. Using a knife, punch a few small holes in the tops of your packets to allow steam to escape.

3. Place on a grill or grate over a medium-high heat, and grill, turning occasionally, until the packet is warmed through and the cheese is melted. This generally takes anywhere from 6–15 minutes depending on how many toppings you are using. Serve with sour cream and salsa.

FIRESIDE QUESO

Oh, what was that? You wanted queso *with* your nachos? I've got ya. I never thought of myself as a queso person, but I am a melted cheese person. So, when my friend Jake explained to me that queso was basically just melted cheese, I hopped on the queso wagon real quick. I like to stir in cream cheese to keep it, well, creamier.

Ingredients

1 tablespoon (15 ml) oil

2 cloves garlic, minced

4 scallions, root end removed, cut into thin slices

1 cup (237 ml) milk

1 teaspoon salt

1 teaspoon chili powder

1 teaspoon cumin

1 cup (120 g) each of shredded Monterey Jack, sharp cheddar, and Colby cheeses (If you are wondering if you can just use 3 cups [345 g] of a shredded "Mexican cheese" blend, YES, go for it! Respect.)

8 ounces (225 g) cream cheese

1 3.5-ounce (100 g) can chopped jalapeño, if desired

Make It

1. In a heavy skillet, heat the oil over medium heat. Add the garlic and scallions and cook until softened, about 2–3 minutes.

2. Turn the heat to low, stir in the milk, and bring to a simmer. Stir in the salt, spices, shredded cheeses, and cream cheese, mixing until smooth—this can take a minute, so just keep going until the shredded cheese is all melted together. Add the jalapeños and stir to incorporate, if you wish. Add more milk as necessary if the queso is too thick. Serve warm with chips, crackers, veggies, or bread. (Queso is fun to use as a dip for the *pinnebrød* on page 102.)

3. Queso will thicken and harden as it cools, because that's just how melted cheese works. Rewarm it and stir in more milk as desired.

CHOOSE YOUR OWN ADVENTURE RAMEN BOWL

Many of the most successful meals in our family are those where I put out all the ingredients to allow each family member to assemble their own version, be it tacos, salads, even soups. Our boys really like to choose their own vegetables and proteins and sprinkle them in. This approach is one way to get them to eat buckets of things such as cabbage, so I don't ask questions, even if it does mean a few extra serving bowls for cleaning after dinner. We use ramen as one such meal. Proper ramen, a traditional Japanese dish, can be made with different kinds of broth as the base, from a lighter miso broth to an incredibly rich pork broth. These traditional stocks often simmer for hours and become transcendently flavorful. To make it camping-friendly, albeit not traditional, we switch to a quick broth that is still nicely savory and definitely a step up from using dehydrated flavor packets! I put the different topping options out separately, and everyone decorates their bowl from there.

recipe continues

Ingredients

FOR THE RAMEN

1 tablespoon (15 ml) sesame oil, or olive oil if you haven't packed sesame oil

½ cup (50 g), sliced scallions

3 garlic cloves, minced

2-inch (5 cm) chunk of fresh ginger, grated

4 chicken or vegetable bouillon cubes (or 4 teaspoons Better Than Bouillon)

4 cups (946 ml) water

2 tablespoons (30 ml) soy sauce

2 tablespoons (30 ml) rice wine vinegar (or white wine vinegar)

1 ounce (28 g) dried shitake mushrooms

3 packets dried ramen noodles, seasoning packets removed

FOR THE TOPPINGS

2 cups (450 g) shredded cooked chicken, prepared at home (or buy a rotisserie chicken and shred it and pack it) and quickly warmed up in a skillet right before serving

One block silken tofu, cut into small cubes

2 soft-boiled eggs, peeled and sliced in half (to cook the eggs, bring a small pot of water to a boil, add the eggs, and cook for 4–8 minutes, depending on how hard-cooked you like them. For quite a soft yolk, cook for 4 minutes; for a fully set yolk, cook for 8 minutes. Once cooked, transfer to cold water to cool before you peel them.)

½ cup (50 g) sliced scallions

1 medium to large carrot, grated

Fresh arugula or watercress

Sriracha or another hot sauce for those who like some spice

Make It

1. In a large pot, heat the oil over high heat and add the scallions. Cook for about 2 minutes, then stir in the garlic and ginger and cook for an additional 1–2 minutes until the garlic is softening.

2. Add the bouillon, water, soy sauce, vinegar, and dried mushrooms. Bring everything to a boil, then lower the heat and simmer the broth for 10–15 minutes until the mushrooms have softened.

3. Add the ramen noodles and cook for 4 more minutes, then remove from the heat.

4. To serve, divide the noodles and broth between four bowls and allow everyone to choose and add their own toppings.

WIDJI'S MEAT AND CHEESE BOARD

Camp Widjiwagan is a canoe camp in Northern Minnesota where many school groups go for an outdoor experience. Large swathes of the population around here have fond memories of going to Widji in fifth or sixth grade, and among those fond memories the meat and cheese board looms large. Cop Widji's style and set out your own meat and cheese board to go with dinner or to have *for* dinner! It's as easy as setting out snacks on a cutting board, but it feels so fancy.

Ingredients

3 types of cheeses, cut into slices if they are hard cheeses (if you're looking for suggestions, consider cheddar, gouda, and brie as your options—they're my personal faves); for 4 people, I suggest about 16 ounces (455 g) of cheese in total

Sliced hard salami, about 2 ounces (55 g) for 4 people

Sliced prosciutto, about 2 ounces (55 g) for 4 people

A small bowl or camp mug filled with nuts

A small bowl or cup filled with olives, if desired

Dried apricots

Grapes

A bunch of crackers

(Feel free to add any other goodies you have on hand that sound good that day)

Make It

1. Set everything out on a large cutting board or plate, arranging them artfully because you're being outdoors fancy here. I start by putting the largest object about a third of the way in from one side. Then I add cheeses, any large bunches of grapes, and any little bowls and cups around the board or plate in a pattern like the seven card in a deck of playing cards or the dots on the five side of a playing die. Use the meats, crackers, and dried fruit to fill in the spaces between the cheeses and bowls.

2. Make sure you have a couple of knives available for slicing. Then let everyone help themselves!

MILENA'S DRIED WILD MUSHROOM RISOTTO

Our friend Milena lives in Austria, but whenever she comes to visit Minnesota, a Boundary Waters trip is on the docket. She's a pro camper and cook, and this is her clever way to take a box of store-bought quick risotto and turn it into an incredibly special meal. My kids happen to love both mushrooms and rice, so this elegant meal suits us to a T.

Ingredients

½ cup (55 g) dried wild mushrooms of your preferred variety (or varieties!)

3 cups (710 ml) warm water

2 tablespoons (30 ml) olive oil

1 small yellow onion, chopped

1 clove garlic, minced

1 box of store-bought quick risotto mix (these are usually 5½–8 ounces [155–225 g] in size)

½ cup (120 ml) white wine (optional, but really good. Replace with broth if you have no wine)

2 teaspoons (10 ml) white wine vinegar or lemon juice

Salt and pepper

Lots of shredded Parmesan cheese (about a cup [100 g])

Make It

1. Combine the dried mushrooms and warm water in a bowl and set aside for about 10 minutes.

2. In a pot, heat the olive oil over medium-high heat, then add the onion and garlic. Cook until the onion is translucent, about 2–3 minutes. Add the rice from the box and stir to coat with the oil, onion, and garlic. Cook for another 2 minutes.

3. Add the wine and a splash of the water from the mushrooms. Allow the wine to cook off and absorb, another 2 minutes.

4. Add the mushrooms and the remaining water from the mushrooms, leaving any sediment in the bottom of the bowl behind. Bring to a simmer, then turn the heat to low and allow to cook until the liquid has almost completely absorbed and the rice is tender.

5. Stir in the vinegar or lemon juice. Season with plenty of salt and pepper. Stir in the Parmesan just before serving.

RICE BOWLS WITH EASY PEANUT SAUCE

Rice bowls are a great way to turn any bits and bobs you have into something that feels like a complete meal. It's a simple but satisfying dinner when you're a few days into camping and have used up most of the fresh things in your cooler.

Ingredients

2 cups (195 g) rice

4 cups (946 ml) water

Salt

2–3 cups (142–213 g) of any vegetables you like, chopped into 1–2-inch (2.5–5 cm) pieces

2 tablespoons (30 ml) olive oil

¾ cup (195 g) peanut butter

3 tablespoons (45 ml) soy sauce

3 tablespoons (45 ml) vinegar (preferably rice vinegar or white wine vinegar, but use what you've got)

3 tablespoons sugar (13 g), brown sugar (45 g), maple syrup (60 g), or honey (60 g)

2 cloves garlic, minced

Sriracha or another favorite hot sauce for serving, if you like

Make It

1. Combine the rice with water and a big pinch of salt in a pot. Bring to a boil, then turn down to a low simmer. Cover and cook until the water is fully absorbed and the rice is tender, about 20 minutes.

2. Meanwhile, sauté your vegetables, if you wish! Heat the olive oil in a skillet over medium-high heat. Add your vegetables, sprinkle with salt, and sauté until your vegetables are lightly tender. The amount of time this takes will depend on the vegetables.

3. To make the easy peanut sauce, whisk together the peanut butter, soy sauce, vinegar, sweetener of choice, and garlic in a small bowl. Thin with water to reach your desired consistency.

4. Divide the cooked rice between four bowls, pile some vegetables on top of each, and spoon on the peanut sauce.

KEBAB FAJITAS

I go through spates of getting sick of food. But no matter how bored I feel of every other food under the sun, tacos and fajitas are always there to come to my rescue. I'm never tired of them. And my boys are always happy to eat them as well because it gives them an excuse to smear sour cream on tortillas. (Have I mentioned they are really into carbs and dairy?) These tacos take a page out of the fajita playbook, complementing the zippy marinated chicken with grilled onion and bell pepper. Assembling the chicken and vegetables onto skewers at home makes it a breeze to get dinner onto the grill when you're in camp.

Ingredients

FOR THE MARINADE

Juice of one lime

2 garlic cloves, minced

½ teaspoon salt

2 teaspoons chili powder

2 teaspoons cumin

FOR THE KEBABS

1 pound (455 g) boneless, skinless chicken thighs, cut into bite-sized (¾-inch [1.9 cm]) chunks

1 red onion, cut into ¾-inch (1.9 cm) chunks

2 bell peppers in different colors, cut into ¾-inch (1.9 cm) chunks

1–2 tablespoons (15–30 ml) olive oil

TO SERVE

Flour tortillas

Sour cream

Cilantro

Sliced avocado

Lime wedges

Make It

AT HOME

1. Whisk together the marinade ingredients, then place in a shallow dish and add the chicken pieces. Toss the chicken to coat. Cover the dish, place it in the refrigerator, and allow to marinate overnight.

2. After the meat has marinated, thread the chicken, onion, and bell pepper chunks on skewers in an alternating pattern. Place skewers in a heavy-duty zip-top bag or sealable container and pack in the coldest part of your cooler.

IN CAMP

1. Brush the kebabs with olive oil. Place the skewers on a grill or grate over a campfire at medium-high heat. Grill, turning occasionally until the vegetables are soft and the meat is cooked through to an internal temperature of 165°F (74°C), about 20 minutes.

2. Serve the kebabs with the tortillas and other toppings so everyone can assemble their own fajitas.

CHICKPEAS AND COUSCOUS

I love using cinnamon in savory dishes, especially combined with other warm, earthy spices such as cumin and paprika, which is exactly the combo in this lovely one-pot vegetarian meal of chickpeas, veggies, and couscous. Think of it as a tagine, but not cooked in a tagine, so really not a tagine at all—but still excellent. A word to the wise: This dish gets even better over time, so you can also make it ahead and eat it cold or reheated for lunch or dinner.

Ingredients

1 teaspoon ground cinnamon

1 teaspoon ground cumin

1 teaspoon sweet paprika

2 tablespoons (30 ml) olive oil

1 shallot, minced

2 large cloves garlic, minced

2 medium carrots, sliced into thin rounds

1 sweet bell pepper, diced

1 large tomato, diced

1 15-ounce (425 g) can chickpeas, drained

1½ cups (355 ml) vegetable broth or 1½ cups (355 ml) water and 1½ cubes vegetable bouillon

1 teaspoon salt

1 cup (157 g) couscous

¼ cup (35 g) golden raisins

Lots of chopped flat-leaf parsley and plain yogurt (optional)

Make It

AT HOME

Combine the spices and put them into a small, sealed container labeled with the meal name.

IN CAMP

1. In a pot, heat the olive oil over medium-high heat until it is shimmering, then stir in the chopped shallot and garlic. Cook the shallot and garlic until they start to soften, about 2 minutes, then stir in the cinnamon, cumin, and paprika and cook until the spices are fragrant, about 1 minute.

2. Add the carrots, bell pepper, and tomato and stir to coat with the spices. Cook the veggies, stirring frequently, for about 5 minutes, then add the chickpeas, broth (or water and bouillon), and salt. Reduce the heat to a simmer and cook for 10 minutes.

3. Turn off the heat, stir in the couscous, and cover the pot. Let it sit for 5 minutes while the couscous absorbs the liquid. Take off the lid and use a fork to stir everything and fluff up the couscous. Put the cover back on and let it sit for 5 more minutes. Stir in the raisins, garnish as desired, and serve!

SIMPLE, WARMING DAHL WITH NO-YEAST SKILLET FLATBREAD

Dahl is a beautifully spiced stew from India that can be made from any number of types of split legumes, ranging from split chickpeas to lentils. Split red lentils cook up remarkably quickly, making red lentil dahl a perfect meal for camping. I like how red lentils break down more than other types of lentils to make a nice mush, because mush makes me think of *Goodnight Moon*, and there is quite possibly nothing more comforting. Quick and easy skillet flatbreads make the perfect pairing, and it's fun to let kids roll out the flatbreads with a water bottle. You can certainly substitute store-bought naan, roti, or rice if you would like, though.

Ingredients

FOR THE DAHL

1 teaspoon turmeric

2 teaspoons madras curry powder

1 teaspoon garam masala

1 teaspoon ground cumin

½ teaspoon ground ginger

2 tablespoons (30 ml) olive oil

1 large onion, chopped

2 garlic cloves, peeled and smashed

1⅔ cups (329 g) split red lentils, rinsed

3¼ cups (770 ml) water

3 vegetable bouillon cubes (optional)

1 large tomato, chopped

1 14.5-ounce (439 ml) can coconut milk

Salt

Plain yogurt, for serving (optional)

Chopped cilantro, for serving (optional)

FOR THE FLATBREAD

1½ cups (188 g) all-purpose flour

1 teaspoon baking powder

¾ teaspoon salt

2 tablespoons (30 ml) olive oil

½ cup (120 ml) water

Make It

TO MAKE THE DAHL

AT HOME
Combine the spices and place them in a small sealed and labeled container.

IN CAMP
1. Heat the olive oil over medium-high heat in a large pot until the oil is shimmering. Add the onion and garlic and cook until softened, about 3 minutes.

recipe continues

2. Stir in the spices and cook until fragrant, about 30 seconds. Then add the lentils and stir to coat with oil and spices. Add the water, bouillon, if using, and chopped tomato, and stir well. Bring to a boil, turn down to a simmer, and cook for 10 minutes or until much of the liquid has been absorbed.

3. Stir in the coconut milk and simmer for another 10 minutes until the lentils are tender. Serve topped with plain yogurt and cilantro if desired. Serve the warm flatbreads or rice on the side.

TO MAKE THE FLATBREADS

1. In a bowl, combine the flour, baking powder, and salt. Stir in the oil and half the water, then continue to stir in water until you have a soft, shaggy dough. In the bowl, knead the dough until it becomes more cohesive, about 1 minute. Cover and set aside to rest for 10 minutes.

2. Start heating a heavy skillet over medium-high heat. Meanwhile, divide the dough into six equal pieces and roll each into a ball. Using a water bottle or other roller, roll the first piece out into a quarter-inch (0.5 cm) thick oval (you can also stretch them by hand like pizza dough, if you want). I usually don't use more flour to roll; I tame dough into submission with confidence, but when the kids roll, we often need to sprinkle extra flour on the roller and the cutting board we use as a surface to avoid too much stickage.

3. Transfer the rolled dough to the skillet and cook for 2–3 minutes per side until it has nice brown-gold marks on each side. If it starts to blacken before 2 minutes on either side, turn down the heat. Transfer to a plate once cooked on both sides.

4. While the first flatbread is cooking, roll out another piece, then fry it after removing the first flatbread and continue the same process until all the flatbreads are cooked.

CHILI WITH CORN BREAD TOPPING

Chili with corn bread is classic. But chili topped with corn bread almost like a hearty, savory cobbler? That's next level! Especially when it's a rather good chili and an almost impossibly fluffy corn bread.

Ingredients

FOR THE CORN BREAD TOPPING

1 cup (126 g) cornmeal

1 cup (125 g) flour

⅓ cup (67 g) sugar

1 teaspoon salt

1 tablespoon (14 g) baking powder

1 egg

1 cup (235 ml) milk, yogurt, or buttermilk

⅓ cup (79 ml) vegetable oil (I often just use olive oil because I always have it)

FOR THE CHILI

2 tablespoons (30 ml) olive oil

1 yellow onion, diced

1 red or yellow bell pepper, diced

1 pound (455 g) ground pork or beef

2 large garlic cloves, minced

1 3.5-ounce (104 g) can jalapeños, chopped (optional, omit this if your kids are like mine and don't like anything spicy no matter how hard you try)

2 tablespoons (15 g) chili powder

1 teaspoon cumin

1 teaspoon dried oregano

2 teaspoons salt

2 tablespoons (30 g) ketchup

1 14.5-ounce (414 g) can crushed tomatoes

1 14.5-ounce (464 g) can pinto beans

Chopped cilantro and sour cream for serving (optional)

SPECIAL EQUIPMENT: a 12-inch (30 cm) Dutch oven or a 10-inch (25 cm) Dutch oven that is deep-sided

recipe continues

Make It

AT HOME

1. Combine all the dry ingredients for the corn bread (cornmeal, flour, sugar, salt, baking powder) in a small, sealed container so you have them ready to go in camp.

2. If you want, you can also combine the chili spices and put them in their own little baggie labeled with "chili spices" so that those are ready to rumble as well.

IN CAMP

1. Put the Dutch oven over the campfire and let it get hot. Add the olive oil and stir in the onion and chopped pepper. Cook, stirring until the onion begins to soften and gets translucent. Next, stir in the ground beef or pork, garlic, jalapeños (if using), spices, and 2 teaspoons salt. Cook, stirring occasionally, until the meat is browned. Then stir in the ketchup, canned tomatoes, and beans. Allow this to simmer for about 10 minutes.

2. While the chili is simmering, combine the corn bread dry ingredients with the egg, milk (or yogurt or buttermilk), and oil and stir until just combined. I like to let my kids help with the corn bread mixing. Remove the chili from the fire and spoon the corn bread batter over the top of it, gently spreading the batter out across the top of the chili to cover as much as possible.

3. Shovel a few of your fire embers or coals off to the side of your fire to make a small ring and place your Dutch oven on top of it. Cover the Dutch oven with its lid, then shovel embers or coals on top of the Dutch oven. (For more in-depth instructions, see the "Dutch Oven Primer," page 25.) Allow to sit for about 20–30 minutes, replacing the embers on top if they get too cold. After 20 minutes, carefully lift the cover and use a knife or skewer to test whether the corn bread is cooked through. Once a knife inserted into the corn bread comes out clean, remove the Dutch oven from the coals, allow to cool for a few minutes, then enjoy!

ONE-PAN PICADILLO

Picadillo is a traditional dish across Latin America as well as the Philippines, with each region (not to mention each family) having their own variation. I learned this Mexican version from my friend Christina and quickly adopted it. The lightly spiced combination of beef, tomatoes, and potatoes makes an excellent stand-alone dish or taco filling that always has my kids clamoring for seconds.

Ingredients

1 tablespoon (15 ml) olive oil

1 small yellow onion, finely chopped

1 green bell pepper, finely chopped

3 garlic cloves, finely chopped

1 teaspoon ground cumin

1 teaspoon ground cinnamon

1 pound (455 g) ground beef

1½ teaspoons salt

1 medium Yukon gold or russet potato, finely diced

3 medium tomatoes, chopped

1 bouillon cube

1 cup (237 ml) water

1 15-ounce (427 g) can corn, drained, or 2 cups (330 g) frozen corn, defrosted

Cilantro for serving (optional)

Make It

1. In a 12-inch (30 cm) cast-iron skillet, heat the olive oil over high heat, then add the onion and bell pepper. Cook, stirring, until the onion is translucent, about 2 minutes.

2. Stir in the garlic, cumin, and cinnamon and cook for about 30 seconds until fragrant, then stir in the ground beef. Cook, breaking apart the beef until the beef is most of the way cooked through, about 5 minutes. Stir in the salt, diced potato, chopped tomatoes, bouillon, and water. When the mixture is simmering, cover and cook for 10 minutes.

3. Remove the cover, stir in the corn, and cook for another 10 minutes or so until the potatoes are tender. Sprinkle with cilantro (if using) and serve with cooked rice or tortillas.

BEEF AND DRIED APRICOT CURRY

This is the most simplified, quick-cooking version of a curry you can possibly imagine. It's a favorite of mine because of the lovely combination of sweet, savory, and aromatic flavors. On the other hand, it's a favorite with my boys because they are dried apricot fanatics. If you prefer, you can make it with ground turkey instead of beef.

Ingredients

1 tablespoon (15 ml) olive oil

1 small yellow onion, finely chopped

2 large carrots, finely diced

3 large cloves garlic, minced

1 tablespoon (6.3 g) curry powder

1 pound (455 g) ground beef (or turkey)

1 cup (237 ml) water

1 beef or vegetable bouillon cube

½ cup (85 g) dried apricots, sliced

Salt and pepper

Make It

1. In a large skillet, heat the oil over medium to high heat. Add the onion and carrots and cook, stirring, until the onion becomes translucent, about 2 minutes. Stir in the garlic and curry powder and cook until fragrant, another 30 seconds to 1 minute.

2. Next, stir in the beef (or turkey) and 1 teaspoon salt. Cook, breaking apart the meat with your cooking spoon, until the meat is browned, about 3–5 minutes.

3. Stir in the water, bouillon cube, and apricots. Cook over medium heat, stirring occasionally, until the sauce has thickened somewhat and the apricot is soft and plump, about 8 minutes. I like to serve this with a side of sautéed cauliflower, while my kids like it with rice (though they like everything with rice).

PITA OR NAAN PIZZAS

Grilling pizza with fresh dough can be super fun, and if you're up for it, I highly recommend it as an activity (with these same topping combos!). But, it can also be stressful and fiddly, with dough tearing and drooping and charring while toddlers run away because dinner is taking too long. For the days, and especially on trips, where you want pizza on the menu but you want to keep it really simple, I recommend taking a classic shortcut and using prepared pita bread or naan breads for crusts. You still get the fun of everyone choosing their toppings and the deliciousness of fresh hot pizza but without having to worry about nailing the crust.

Ingredients

4 store-bought pitas or naan breads

1 24-ounce (735 g) jar tomato sauce (you won't need the whole jar, so you can use the remainder to make eggs in purgatory [page 70] the next morning!)

TOPPINGS

Pepperoni

Canned pineapple pieces (save the leftover juice for pineapple basil gimlets, page 184)

Shredded mozzarella

A few wheels of very thinly sliced lemon, peel on

Prosciutto

Sliced green olives

Fresh mozzarella

Fresh basil

Olive oil

Make It

1. Place a cast-iron skillet (or another heavy skillet) on a grill over medium heat. Let the skillet get warm.

2. For each pizza, place a pita or naan into the skillet and let the first side toast for 1 minute. Flip, then quickly add toppings and cover the pan. Allow the pizza to cook until the cheese is melted, then transfer to a plate. Repeat the process with each of the remaining pitas/naans until everyone has a pizza.

PIZZA TOPPING COMBO 1

Pizza sauce, pepperoni, canned pineapple chunks, olive slices, and shredded mozzarella. Sprinkle on fresh basil after the pizza is cooked.

PIZZA TOPPING COMBO 2 (AKA MY PIZZA)

Thinly sliced pieces of lemon, a little prosciutto, olive slices, slices of fresh mozzarella, and a drizzle of olive oil. Sprinkle on fresh basil after the pizza is cooked.

TIPS: In general, I would say go ahead and assemble your pizza however you want to, but as a word of warning, I will also say don't go too overboard on the amount of pizza sauce or cheese, or it will be hard to get the cheese hot and melty without burning the bottom of the pizza.

ITALIAN SAUSAGE BURGERS WITH GRILLED VEG

Before my husband and I got married, a few friends had a bachelorette party for me in Portland, Maine. It was the most wholesome bachelorette party you can possibly imagine, including apple picking, braiding flower crowns, and then having a very nice meal at a fancy restaurant and going to bed early. Basically my idea of heaven. Meanwhile, my husband and his friend Jamie kayaked to an island where Jamie—who is a fantastic cook—cooked Suzanne Goin's pork and chorizo burgers with romesco and aioli. In spite of my gourmet meal, I have to admit I was jealous of their burgers. That means I had to take Suzanne's pork burgers for a spin not long afterward, and I must say they are genius. They also instilled in me an interest in figuring out how to make spiced pork burgers that don't take 57 separate steps to execute. Cue Italian sausage.

We make quarter-pound (113 g) burgers, but feel free to increase the amount of meat to a pound and a half (680 g) for four burgers if you like them a little larger. For vegetarians, use thick slices of fresh mozzarella instead of the sausage burgers and serve the mozzarella slices with grilled vegetables and basil aioli on ciabatta buns.

Ingredients

1 pound (454 g) bulk mild Italian sausage (squeeze sausage out of casings if you can't find it in bulk)

2 small zucchini, sliced horizontally into long ¼-inch (0.5 cm) thick slices

1 large, sturdy tomato (such as beefsteak), cored and cut into 4 thick rounds

Juice of one lemon, divided

Olive oil

Salt and pepper

¼ cup (60 g) mayonnaise

2 tablespoons (5 g) chopped fresh basil

1 small garlic clove, minced

4 ciabatta buns, split

Make It

AT HOME

1. Divide the sausage into four equal portions and gently form the sausage into patties. Place the patties on a baking tray lined with parchment paper and place them in the freezer to freeze solid, at least 12 hours.

2. Place the frozen patties into a zip-top freezer bag with a piece of parchment paper between each patty. Place the sealed bag inside another bag. Keep the patties frozen until you leave and pack them into your cooler still frozen. They will defrost over time in the cooler, so they will be ready to cook while you are in camp.

recipe continues

A SIDE OF CORN

Since you're grilling, you might want to throw on some cobs of corn as well. We usually grill our corn by peeling back the husk, removing the silk, and then folding the husk back over the cob. Then we just throw the corn onto a high-heat section of the grill and cook until the kernels inside turn bright yellow, about 10 to 15 minutes.

IN CAMP

1. Heat your grill or your campfire with a grate over it and allow the fire to burn down to medium-hot embers.

2. Brush the zucchini slices on both sides with olive oil and half of the lemon juice and sprinkle with salt and pepper. Brush the tomato slices with olive oil and sprinkle with salt and pepper as well.

3. Put your sausage patties on the grill and cook, flipping occasionally, until completely cooked through, about 4–5 minutes per side.

4. At the same time, grill the zucchini slices and tomato slices until soft, about 4–5 minutes per side.

5. In a bowl, stir together the mayonnaise, chopped basil, minced garlic, and remaining lemon juice. Season with salt to taste.

6. Lightly toast the ciabatta buns. Assemble the burgers by spreading each bun with the basil aioli, top it with a sausage patty, a couple zucchini slices, and a slice of tomato and then close with the other half of the bun. Serve any remaining zucchini on the side.

FOIL-BAKED SWEET POTATOES WITH FILLINGS

You know what's even better than a baked potato? A baked sweet potato. Our family straight up *lives* off sweet potatoes. If you took away sweet potatoes, you would remove somewhere in the realm of 75 percent of the bulk of our diet. And while they seem boldly flavored—certainly compared to something mild and starchy such as a russet—their sweet creaminess actually works as the perfect foil to all sorts of other flavors. Just make sure you get enough salt and fat in there because salt + fat + sweet potatoes = a party. I'm giving you two topping options, but honestly, you could go wild with almost anything your heart desires (bacon, for example, or taco toppings, chili, barbecued chicken, the list goes on).

Wrap your sweet potatoes well in foil and you can bake them in the embers of a campfire. They do take a bit of time to cook through, so this is a dinner to make when you have planned ahead, everyone has fun in-camp activities, and you have a box of wine at your side.

Ingredients

FOR THE SWEET POTATOES

4 medium sweet potatoes, washed

Aluminum foil

Butter or olive oil

Salt

TOPPING OPTION 1 (VEGETARIAN)

¼ cup (59 ml) olive oil

1 yellow onion, thinly sliced

2 cloves garlic, thinly sliced

1 15-ounce (428 g) can chickpeas, drained

1 teaspoon turmeric

1 teaspoon sweet paprika

1 pinch red pepper flakes (if you like a little heat; omit if you don't)

Salt

Plain full-fat yogurt

Chopped cilantro (am I starting to seem like a one-trick pony with my insistence on adding yogurt and herbs to things?)

TOPPING OPTION 2 (NOT VEGETARIAN)

1 tablespoon (15 ml) olive oil

1 yellow onion, chopped

8 ounces (225 g) precooked andouille sausage, cut into cubes

A few handfuls of baby spinach (around 4 ounces [115 g])

Salt

Sour cream, if you want to get a little ridiculous about it

Make It

Poke each sweet potato all over with a fork. This makes little holes in the skin to let steam escape and prevent exploding. Wrap each sweet potato in 2 or 3 layers of aluminum foil, sealing each layer well by rolling the edges over themselves. Nestle your sweet potatoes into the embers of your campfire (either of a campfire that has burned low or along the outer edges of a fire). Allow them to bake there,

recipe continues

turning occasionally, until they are soft throughout. This will take around 45 minutes for medium-sized sweet potatoes, but it really depends on the heat of your embers and the size of your potatoes. Remove from the embers (wear heat-resistant gloves or use tongs), open the aluminum wrapping, and let the potatoes cool for a couple minutes until you can handle them enough to slice them open down the middle. Slightly smash up the potatoes in the skins, sprinkle with salt, and either drizzle with olive oil or add a little bit of butter before adding your chosen topping.

FOR TOPPING 1

1. Heat the olive oil in a large skillet over medium-high heat, then add the onion. Cook until the onion is softened and browning around the edges, about 3–5 minutes. Stir in the garlic, chickpeas, and spices and sprinkle with a bit of salt. Cook, stirring occasionally to make sure everything is cooking evenly, for about 10 minutes until everything has nicely browned and looks caramelized. Taste and add more salt if needed.

2. Scoop the chickpea mixture into the sliced-open sweet potatoes. Top with a dollop of plain yogurt and sprinkle generously with chopped cilantro.

FOR TOPPING 2

1. Heat the oil in a large skillet over medium-high heat, then add the onion. Cook until well browned, about 5 minutes.

2. Stir in the chopped andouille sausage and cook for a couple more minutes, stirring occasionally, until the sausage has started to brown on its sides. At the last minute, stir in the spinach and cook until it has just partially wilted, only 30 or so seconds. Season with salt if desired.

3. Scoop the sausage mixture into the sliced-open sweet potatoes. Top each with an additional dollop of sour cream, if desired.

SQUASH AND APPLE FOIL PACKS

Call it the pumpkin spice effect, but when the weather turns crisper, I start to crave winter squash all the time. The mellow sweetness is versatile and delicious. I use squash in myriad ways, but the combination of roasted squash with apples is one I return to time and again because it never fails to be comforting and good. This is an especially perfect side dish for brats.

Ingredients

Aluminum foil

2 cups (280 g) butternut squash, peeled and cut into 1-inch (2.5 cm) cubes

1 cup (150 g) apple, cored and cut into 1-inch (2.5 cm) cubes

4 whole cloves garlic in the skin

Olive oil

2 sprigs of fresh thyme or a couple pinches of dried thyme

Salt

Make It

1. Lay out two pieces of aluminum foil that are approximately 12" x 24" (30 x 60 cm). Divide the squash, apple, and garlic cloves between the two pieces of foil.

2. Drizzle everything well with olive oil, sprinkle with salt and thyme, and then mound the squash and apple mixture toward the center of each aluminum piece. Fold them into packets, then wrap each packet in a second layer of foil.

3. Place the foil packets into the coals and ashes of a fire that has burned down or in the ashes a ways off to the side of an active fire. Allow to bake for 25–35 minutes, or until the squash is completely tender. Remove from the fire using long tongs, allow to cool until the edges of the tinfoil can be handled, then open the packets. Squeeze the garlic cloves out of their skins and mix them into the squash and apples. Serve warm as an accompaniment to sausage.

TIP: High summer instead of early fall? Use the same technique but combine quartered nectarines with sliced sweet onions for another amazing, sweet-savory side for grilled sausages.

CHAPTER FIVE

TREATS
and
DRINKS

❖

Is it a good idea to dose the kids up with sugar before zipping them into a tent and expecting them to sleep? No, probably not. Is it mandatory anyway? Yes. When you are sitting around a campfire, singing songs, and telling stories, you simply can't get away with not making a sweet treat and enjoying some sweet drinks. It is part of the camping weekend brief. Embrace it.

S'MORES GALORES!

We all know that the real reason to go camping is to make s'mores. Let's not even try to pretend otherwise. There's something eerily perfect about the classic combination of graham cracker, toasted marshmallow, and milk chocolate. Why is it so very good? What secrets is it hiding? But, perfection can be embellished to great effect, and all sorts of variations on s'mores fillings exist. Try dark chocolate instead of milk. Add sliced strawberries or a smear of peanut butter or use chocolate hazelnut spread instead of chocolate! But, then I got to thinking, why stop at the fillings? Aren't the outsides of the s'more also ripe for innovation? The answer is yes, and the following are some excellent (and decadent) options. But, if you want to stick with the original, that's okay too, because why mess with perfection?

Make It

CHOCOLATE MINT S'MORE

Use two crispy chocolate icebox cookies, put an Andes mint or two on one, add a toasted marshmallow, and smoosh the other cookie on top.

CHOCOLATE CHIP COOKIE S'MORE

Make a s'more with two chocolate chip cookies, a piece of dark chocolate, and a toasted marshmallow. We actually make these quite often, and they are ridiculously decadent and totally awesome.

GINGERSNAP S'MORE

Use two gingersnaps and add a piece of milk chocolate and a piece of crystallized ginger to one. Add a toasted marshmallow and smoosh the other gingersnap on top.

LEMON MERINGUE PIE S'MORE

Okay, we are back to graham crackers on this one, but it's still innovative. Spread a graham cracker with lemon curd (you can also put lemon curd on biscuits or pancakes!), top with a toasted marshmallow, then smoosh another graham cracker on top.

DEVIL'S FOOD S'MORE

Smoosh your toasted marshmallow with a piece of chocolate between two soft-baked chocolate cookies. Use store-bought cookies or try the recipe that follows.

SOFT CHOCOLATE COOKIES

I created this recipe especially for wedging toasted marshmallows between to make a sort of devil's food/whoopee pie s'more situation. But, they are also amazing for snacking, or for making decadent ice cream sandwiches when you are at home. The combination of salt and chocolate is irresistible.

Ingredients

6 tablespoons (85 g) butter, softened

¾ cup (170 g) light brown sugar

1 egg

1 teaspoon vanilla extract

1 cup (125 g) flour

⅓ cup (29 g) cocoa powder

½ teaspoon baking soda

¼ teaspoon salt

1 tablespoon (15 ml) whole milk

Flaky salt for sprinkling

Make It

AT HOME

1. Preheat the oven to 350°F (180°C, or gas mark 4). In the bowl of a stand mixer fitted with a paddle attachment (or using a hand mixer), cream the butter and brown sugar together until lightened in color, about 3 minutes. Add the egg and beat in until fully incorporated.

2. In a small bowl, sift together the flour, cocoa powder, baking soda, and salt (normally I don't bother with sifting dry ingredients, but it's helpful to do with cocoa powder as it tends to clump). Add the dry ingredients to the butter-sugar mixture and mix on low speed until almost fully combined. Add the milk and continue to mix just until everything is a uniform color and texture.

3. Scoop the dough into rounded tablespoon-sized balls and place onto a baking sheet. Sprinkle each with a small pinch of flaky salt. Bake for 9–10 minutes until they look puffed and dry on top but are still very pillowy and soft to the touch. Remove from the oven, transfer to a cooling rack, and allow to cool completely. (Okay, yes, you probably want to snack on one while it's still warm.) Transfer the cookies into an airtight container to pack for camping.

BANANA BOATS

You could camp without making banana boats, but are you really camping then? Banana boats are a camping dessert that is *allllmost* as classic as s'mores. And they are equally fun and sticky.

Ingredients

Bananas still in their skins

Assorted fillings (see below)

Aluminum foil

Make It

1. Cut a slit down the middle of each banana, making sure you don't pierce through the skin on the bottom. Stuff the slit full of the filling combination of your choice (see below), then wrap your banana in two layers of aluminum foil.

2. Place the foil-wrapped bananas on a grate over the fire or settle them directly on dying embers. Cook until the bananas are soft and the fillings are melted, about 15–20 minutes.

3. Use long tongs to take the bananas off the fire, allow the aluminum to cool for just a minute, then unwrap the bananas and enjoy them while they are still a hot, sticky mess. I recommend eating them out of their peels with a spoon.

FILLING COMBINATIONS!

- **THE CLASSIC:** chocolate chips and mini marshmallows (or regular marshmallows torn to bits)

- **THE BANANAS FOSTER (FOR ADULTS ONLY!):** brown sugar, a pat of butter, and a small spoonful of rum or bourbon

- **THE BANANA SPLIT:** chocolate chips, sliced strawberries, and canned pineapple bits

- **THE TROPICAL:** marshmallow bits, canned pineapple bits, and toasted shredded coconut

- **THE STICKY BUN:** caramel sauce, toasted pecans, and a sprinkle of sea salt

- **THE PB:** peanut butter, honey, and graham cracker bits

CAMPFIRE COBBLER

Based on the southern cuppa-cuppa-cuppa-style cobbler, this is my method for making a cakelike dessert when I don't bring a Dutch oven. The butter melted into the pan before adding the batter will seep over the sides of the pan, creating an amazing caramelized crispy chewiness while the berries cook into intense pops of flavor—yet the center stays soft and barely set.

Ingredients

1 cup (125 g) flour

1 ½ teaspoons (7 g) baking powder

½ teaspoon salt

1 cup (200 g) sugar

8 tablespoons (112 g) butter

1 cup (237 ml) whole milk

1 teaspoon vanilla

2 cups (290 g) fresh blueberries

Make It

1. Whisk together the flour, baking powder, salt, and sugar. This step can also be done at home and the premixed dry ingredients can be packed in a sealed container for transport to camp.

2. Place a 9-inch (23 cm), heavy-bottomed heat-resistant skillet (such as cast iron) on a grate over a campfire that has burned down to hot embers (or place the grate off to the side of an active fire). Add the stick of butter to the skillet and allow it to melt completely.

3. Add the milk and vanilla to the dry ingredients and stir together until smooth. With big oven mitts or heat-resistant leather gloves, grab the pan handle and swirl the hot pan with the butter to make sure it is fully coating the pan in a thick layer. Pour in the batter you made. As the batter sloshes into the pan, the butter will creep up all around the edges and over the top of the batter in some places.

4. Scatter the blueberries over the top of the batter, cover, and cook until the batter has just barely set in the middle, around 35 minutes. The bottom will most likely get burned (I don't think I've ever not burned it), but we all really like the burned bottom because it is deliciously caramelized from the butter.

5. Remove the cobbler from the fire and serve warm.

CARAMELIZED APPLE CRUMBLE

I love sizzling fruit in a skillet to make a fast, caramelized fruit dessert. Almost any fruit works well, but apples are my favorite because this recipe creates something that is not far off in flavor from apple pie, but with islands of butterscotch topping floating on top. The granola is optional, but it adds a nice crunchy counterpoint to the soft fruit.

Ingredients

6 tablespoons (85 g) salted butter, divided

½ cup (63 g) flour

½ cup (115 g) brown sugar

5 sweet-tart apples (such as Pink Lady, Braeburn, or Granny Smith), cored and cut into thin slices

½ cup (96 g) granola (optional [page 34])

Make It

1. In a small bowl, rub together 4 tablespoons (55 g) of butter with the flour and brown sugar until it looks like wet crumbs.

2. Place a large cast-iron (or heavy-bottomed) skillet over medium-high heat, or over a fire with medium-hot embers. Add 2 tablespoons (28 g) of butter to the skillet and let it melt. Add the apples and cook, stirring frequently, until the apples have started to brown and caramelize, around 5–7 minutes.

3. Move the pan to a slightly lower heat zone or turn the heat down to medium. If the apples seem dry, stir in a couple of tablespoons of water or bourbon. Sprinkle the butter-flour-sugar mixture over the top of the apples, cover the pan, and cook until the crumble mixture has turned butterscotchy and has set on the top, another 5–10 minutes.

4. Remove the crumble from the heat and sprinkle granola over the top for extra crunch.

REALLY QUICK APPLE CRUNCH

Need an even faster and easier apple dessert? One of my favorite things to do is to crush gingersnaps and sprinkle them over applesauce for a little sweet something. Drizzle on a touch of heavy cream, if you like. So simple, so tasty!

CRACKER CRUST PUDDING PIE

This is my answer to our neighbor Sherry's complaint that when they try to make pudding while camping, it never sets. You could say this pudding pie is closer to a ganache pie, as the chocolate is splendidly rich and luxurious, which is just how our family likes it. We aren't lightweights in the chocolate department, and neither is this dessert.

Ingredients

FOR THE CRUST

5 tablespoons (70 g) butter

1½ cups (108 g) butter cracker crumbs (such as Ritz crackers. I like to use salty crackers for the contrast against the sweet, but graham crackers will also totally work.)

¼ cup (50 g) sugar

FOR THE FILLING

1 14.5-ounce (439 ml) can coconut milk, divided

½ teaspoon salt

¼ cup (50 g) sugar

6 ounces (168 g) dark chocolate, finely chopped (or 6 ounces [168 g] dark chocolate chips)

3 tablespoons (24 g) cornstarch

1 teaspoon vanilla

NOTE: A skin will form on top of the pie as it sets, unless you want to lay some plastic wrap directly over the filling. I usually just let it form a skin and save on plastic usage. This is a pudding pie that is better for scooping than trying to make neat slices. The pudding itself sets into a ganachelike consistency and contains itself well, but the crust is pretty crumbly.

Make It

MAKE THE CRUST

In a 9-inch (23 cm) skillet, heat the butter over medium-high heat and cook until it has melted, foamed, and started to turn a nutty brown and smell deliciously fragrant. Remove from the heat and mix in the cracker crumbs and sugar, stirring well to combine. Allow to cool slightly, then use your fingers or a spoon to press the crumbs into an even(ish) layer across the bottom and up the sides of the skillet. Set aside.

MAKE THE FILLING

1. Add two-thirds of the coconut milk to a pot with salt and sugar. Heat over medium heat until steaming. Remove from the heat, add the chocolate, and let it stand for 1 minute, then stir until the chocolate is melted and fully mixed in.

2. In a camp cup or small bowl, stir together the cornstarch and remaining coconut milk to make a slurry. Scrape this slurry into the pot of warm chocolate-coconut mixture and stir to combine.

3. Put the pot back on the stove and cook over medium heat, stirring constantly, until the mixture thickens to a pudding texture. Remove from the heat, stir in the vanilla, then pour the pudding into the cracker crust. Set aside to cool to air temperature, then enjoy (you actually could eat it warm if you want, but it tastes *extra* rich when it's warm).

GRILLED FRUIT

Perhaps for some reason you want a sweet treat that isn't s'mores. Well, grilled fruit is definitely the answer. Magical things happen when flames kiss fruit sugars and caramelize them. Think fruit upside-down cake, without having to turn upside down or mix up a cake. Most fruits are grillable. Cut fruits such as pears, peaches, figs, and bananas in half or into thick slices. This also works with larger fruits such as pineapple and watermelon. Thread small fruits like strawberries or cherries onto skewers.

I suggest stone fruit such as plums, peaches, nectarines, apricots; pineapple slices; bananas (if you didn't banana boat them); or skewers of strawberries.

Place ripe fruit of your preferred variety over indirect heat on your grill grate. Cook, undisturbed, on the first sides until the bottoms of the fruit are caramelizing, usually around 4 minutes. Flip and repeat on the second side.

DUTCH OVEN STRAWBERRY CAKE

This cake is something of an oddball, with a texture that falls somewhere between a cake and a bar that's nice for cutting and eating in hand-held wedges. It's chewy yet light, dotted with soft strawberries like tiny bites of pie, and disappears in a flash as soon as it is cool enough to eat. You could also make this with chopped peaches instead of strawberries.

Ingredients

1 cup (125 g) flour

½ teaspoon baking soda

1 teaspoon cinnamon

¼ teaspoon salt

¼ cup (59 ml) vegetable oil or olive oil

1 cup (200 g) sugar

1 egg

2 cups (340 g) strawberries, hulled and quartered

SPECIAL EQUIPMENT: a 10-inch (25 cm) Dutch oven

Make It

1. In a medium bowl mix together the flour, baking soda, cinnamon, and salt. This can be done ahead of time at home and transported to your campsite in a sealed container labeled with the recipe name.

2. In a bowl, whisk together the vegetable or olive oil and sugar, then add the egg and whisk until smooth. Stir in the flour mixture just until incorporated, making a thick batter. Fold in the strawberries.

3. Butter a 10-inch (25 cm) Dutch oven or line the Dutch oven with parchment paper. Spread the cake dough into the Dutch oven.

4. Cover the Dutch oven with its lid and either place it on a grate over coals or create a ring of coals on a heat-resistant surface and set the Dutch oven directly on top. Shovel more coals onto the top of the Dutch oven. Allow the cake to bake until a tester inserted into it comes out clean, around 20 minutes. You will have to add new hot coals to the lid and bottom 1–2 times during this baking time. (For more specific directions on Dutch oven cooking, refer to the "Dutch Oven Primer," page 25) When the cake is done, carefully take it off the heat, remove the lid, and allow it to cool for a bit before serving.

GOOEY CHOCOLATE DUTCH OVEN CAKE

This is my friend Carin's recipe for Swedish *kladdkake*. One of the most beloved desserts in Sweden, *kladdkake* translates to "gooey cake." And gooey it is. I would say this cake shares about 99.9 percent of its DNA with a bowl of brownie batter. Cake is almost a misnomer because it gives you a dessert more like a baked pudding. Swedes will tell you to err on the side of underbaked rather than overbaked, which is a nice thing for camp cooking because it gives you a sizable margin of error for declaring triumph.

Ingredients

1¼ cups (250 g) sugar

¼ cup (31 g) malted milk powder

½ teaspoon salt

1 cup minus 2 tablespoons (112 g) flour

¼ cup (22 g) cocoa powder

1½ sticks butter (12 tablespoons [170 g])

3 eggs

SPECIAL EQUIPMENT: a 10-inch (25 cm) Dutch oven

Make It

AT HOME

Mix together the sugar, malted milk powder, salt, flour, and cocoa powder. Transfer to a sealed container and label with the recipe name.

IN CAMP

1. In a sauce pot, heat the butter over medium heat until it melts (this can be done over a fire or camp stove). Remove the butter from the heat and stir in the cocoa powder mixture until is well combined. It will be thick.

2. Allow to cool for a few minutes, then whisk in the eggs one at a time until fully incorporated.

3. Butter and line your Dutch oven with parchment paper. Scrape the chocolate batter into the Dutch oven and put the lid on.

4. Place the Dutch oven over the grate of a low fire or create a ring of coals on a heat-resistant surface and place the Dutch oven on top. Shovel coals onto the lid of the Dutch oven to cover. Bake until the cake is bubbly and dry looking on top, but still fudgy in the middle; this usually takes about 20–30 minutes, depending on the heat of the coals. It won't fully set, so the main thing to watch for is that you don't burn the bottom. If you catch the scent of burning chocolate, get the cake off the heat.

5. Remove the cake from the heat and remove the lid. Allow the cake to cool and set for about an hour before eating. Or don't. Swedes are divided as to whether you should eat *kladdkake* warm, room temperature, or cold. So, I guess you do you! Just know that the warmer it is, the gooier and richer it is.

TEA AND HOT CHOCOLATE KIT

You can't camp without hot beverage options. You just can't. Even in midsummer, the air can have a chill in the morning or evening. And if it doesn't, it's still soothing to have a cup of cocoa or chamomile tea by the fire before trying to convince certain people to stop whispering and wiggling and actually go to sleep. I like to have a sealed container with several packets of each of the following.

Ingredients

Powdered hot cocoa (see below for a recipe if you want to make your own from scratch)

Chamomile tea

Mint tea

Red berry or hibiscus tea

Chai (for the morning, if anyone wants it)

DIY HOT COCOA MIX

There are many, many great recipes out there for making your own hot chocolate mix, but here is the one I use because I have a deep-seated love of malt!

Ingredients

3 ounces (85 g) mini chocolate chips

⅔ cup (58 g) cocoa powder

½ cup (62 g) powdered milk

¼ cup (31 g) malted milk powder

¾ cup (150 g) sugar

Pinch of salt

Make It

1. Mix all the ingredients together and transfer to a jar or other airtight container.

2. To make a cup of hot cocoa, add 2–3 tablespoons (10–15 g) of the mix to a mug. Top with 1 cup (237 ml) hot water or hot milk for a rich hot cocoa, allow to stand for a minute to let the chocolate chips melt, and then stir well to combine everything. (If you are a grown-up, you might want to spice your hot cocoa with brandy, bourbon, or peppermint schnapps. Or aquavit if you are super cool and brought aquavit to make the northern daiquiri! Aquavit in hot cocoa is all kinds of stupendous.)

FRENCH PRESS DIRTY CHAI

Dirty chai is a favorite treat for both my husband and me. Although it's a little bit of a doomsday treat, as in, "No one slept and the end is near but it's okay because the sun is out and I'm drinking coffee and tea and sugar at the same time." We don't drink it with breakfast, but use it instead as a 10 a.m. pick-me-up when we are between breakfast coffee and lunch coffee.

Ingredients

⅓ cup (27 g) coarsely ground coffee

4 tablespoons (8 g) loose leaf chai, or 4 bags of chai

1½ cups (355 ml) boiling hot water

1½ cups (355 ml) milk (I prefer whole milk or coconut milk)

2 tablespoons (40 g) maple syrup, or more or less to taste

SPECIAL EQUIPMENT: a camping French press

Make It

1. Put the ground coffee and the tea in the bottom of your French press. (If using tea bags, open them and empty the tea into the French press. You'll likely wind up with tea dust in your drink since bag tea is finer, but that's okay.) Pour the hot water in, allow to steep for about 7 minutes, then press.

2. While the coffee and tea are steeping, gently warm your milk.

3. Divide the coffee-tea mixture into two mugs, add a tablespoon (20 g) of maple syrup to each mug, and stir to dissolve. Pour warm milk into each mug. Enjoy!

RASPBERRY APPLE CIDER

This genius cider comes from my friend, Annie, who lives on a gorgeous organic farm just south of us. Our families have had a lot of winter bonfires where she served us this magical hot cider. "Magical" truly is the only word to describe it. Finally I asked her what her secret was, and the answer was raspberries! The berry notes of raspberry flesh out the apple cider's sweetness and the whole thing is a bit like a drinkable pie in the best possible way.

Ingredients

4 cups (946 ml) apple cider

1 cup (250 g) frozen raspberries

Make It

Heat the cider and raspberries together in a pot over low heat. Keep them warm for about 20–30 minutes to let the raspberry flavor mingle with the apple. You could strain out the raspberries, but really I think it's great with them in there. Serve warm. Grown-ups, feel free to spike this with whiskey, brandy, or rum!

MULLED WINE CONCENTRATE

MAKES PLENTY

Depending on how heavy-handed you like to be, it's enough for turning 2–3 bottles of wine into mulled wine, one happy mug at a time.

I love, love, love mulled wine. It reminds me of happy holiday memories and Thanksgiving camping trips to Maine (chilly and beautiful!). But, the issue with mulled wine is that for it to be really good, you need the spices to steep in the wine over low heat for a long time, preferably a couple hours. And sometimes that's fine because you can have a pot going on the edge of your fire grate while you cook and do other things. But sometimes you want instant gratification, or you want to be able to make a single serving instead of a whole pot. At least, I know I do. That's why I developed this mulled wine concentrate, which is basically a simple syrup infused with mulling spices. Armed with this, you can simply warm a mug of wine, stir in concentrate to taste, and your bliss is at hand.

Ingredients

1 cup (200 g) sugar

1 cup (237 ml) water

1 teaspoon cloves

1 tablespoon (8 g) cardamom pods

2 cinnamon sticks

1-inch (2.5 cm) fresh ginger, grated

Peel of 1 lemon, pith removed with a vegetable peeler

1 orange cut in half

1 teaspoon citric acid (or juice of one lemon)

Make It

AT HOME

1. Combine all the ingredients except the citric acid in a saucepan. Bring to a simmer and cook for 20 minutes.

2. Strain through a fine-mesh strainer and stir the citric acid or lemon juice into the syrup. Allow to cool, then transfer to a leak-proof container and refrigerate until you are packing. Pack in your drinks cooler or keep with your pantry ingredients, but don't leave it uncooled for more than 2–3 days.

IN CAMP

Gently warm red wine, cider, or unsweetened cranberry juice (for an NA version) in a pot until it is steaming but not boiling, then add the mulled wine concentrate to taste. Ladle the warm spiced wine into mugs to enjoy.

FRUIT-INFUSED WATER

In a moment of ill-founded ambition, I once thought maybe I could figure out how to make homemade powdered lemonade and fruit drinks without any weird stuff in them. Spoiler alert, I failed. I mean, sure, you can mix citric acid and sugar and fruit flavorings, but to be honest, it's still kind of weird. You know what's not at all weird and still totally delicious? Fruit-infused water. My kids love, love, love how special having water infused with their favorite fruits feels and tastes, and they actually like that fruit water isn't sugary. Hop on board because the train is headed for hydration station! (Yes, yes, I did just say that. And my kids rolled their eyes so hard they almost tipped over.)

Ingredients

4 cups (946 ml) of water

½–1 cup (87.5–175 g) your choice of mix of fruits, sliced or lightly crushed to allow them to better infuse the water. See our favorite flavor suggestions below!

1 large sprig or 2 small sprigs of a fresh herb (optional; I am pro herb, but my kids are not. Try mint, basil, rosemary, or thyme if you are pro.)

Make It

Combine the water and fruit pieces (and herbs if using) in a jar, place in your cooler, and allow to steep for about 3 hours. Because of the steep time, this is a great thing to start in the morning and drink at lunch or in the afternoon! You can steep for longer, but don't go more than 24 hours.

OUR FAVORITE FRUITS/ COMBINATIONS

- Strawberries and cucumbers
- Watermelon and sometimes mint
- Lemon slices and raspberries
- Orange slices and strawberries
- Pineapple pieces and peach slices
- Grapefruit, lime slices, and mint (okay, I'm the only one who likes this one. But it's so refreshing!)

SUMMER FRUIT CUP

This fun drink takes the British penchant for gin and Pimm's cocktails that are practically fruit salad and sends it in a nonalcoholic direction so everyone can enjoy!

Ingredients

8 slices cucumber

8 strawberries, hulled and halved

1 lemon, cut into 8 slices

2 cans sparkling lemonade

2 cans ginger beer

4 sprigs of mint

Make It

1. Divide the cucumbers, strawberries, and lemon slices evenly between 4 cups. Gently press on the fruit in each cup with the back of a wooden spoon to lightly muddle, but don't smash them up to a pulp or anything.

2. Fill each cup halfway with sparkling lemonade and top with ginger beer. If you have ice, add a few cubes to each cup. Garnish each with a sprig of mint.

THOUGHTS ON "THE CAMPING BAR"

Okay, so technically I have so many thoughts on the camping bar I wrote a book on it. See *Camp Cocktails*, by yours truly. I love having a nice glass of wine or a good cocktail in the woods. I think it elevates the experience and enjoyment of the great outdoors to new levels. And if you're camping with your family, you totally deserve it.

On the packables front, I like to premix several servings of a stirred drink such as a Manhattan or Boulevardier at home and bring it in a jar, Nalgene, or flask to share. You can complement this by bringing a bottle or flask of your favorite base spirit (gin, whiskey, rum...) plus citrus, fruit, and sugar to make fruitier drinks. These days you can also find an assortment of quite good canned cocktails (I make some myself at our distillery!) that make having a cocktail as easy as cracking open a can.

Speaking of, canned wines have come a long way, so it's not a bad idea to ask your liquor store for their canned wine recommendations and pack a couple of those plus some craft beer in your cooler.

All this said, there are as many reasons not to drink alcohol as there are to drink it, and whatever your reason, I think it's great. Most of the drink recipes I've shared up to now are nonalcoholic or can be and are good for anyone to enjoy! But on the pages that follow, I am including a few for adults only.

PINEAPPLE BASIL GIMLET

If your misguided family insists on putting pineapple on their pizza while you prefer mozzarella and basil, (a) you are in good company, and (b) you deserve to make this cocktail with the leftover pineapple juice and basil. If you happen to like pineapple on your pizza . . . ugh, fine, you can have a cocktail too.

Ingredients

1 tablespoon (13 g) sugar

½ ounce (14 ml) lime juice

4 basil leaves

1 ounce (28 ml) pineapple juice (you have it left over from pizza!)

2 ounces (60 ml) gin

Make It

In a shaker, jar, Nalgene, or other sealable container, combine the sugar and lime juice and swirl until the sugar dissolves. Add the basil and muddle it with a spoon. Add the pineapple juice and gin plus a handful of ice. Seal the container and shake really hard for 10 seconds. Pour the drink into a cup and enjoy!

Pineapple Basil Gimlet ▶

NORTHERN DAIQUIRI

I make cocktails for a living and I'm often still shocked at how good the classic three-ingredient cocktails are. This cold-weather cousin of the daiquiri is one such cocktail, and a textbook example of "more than the sum of its parts." Aquavit is a traditional Scandinavian caraway-flavored spirit. We make one at our distillery, and it's one of my favorite spirits to use in cocktails. You can find dill aquavit but use a caraway-dominant one for this cocktail.

Ingredients

2 ounces (60 ml) Aquavit

¾ ounce (21 ml) maple syrup

¾ ounce (21 ml) lime juice

Make It

Combine the ingredients in a shaker, jar, Nalgene, or other sealable container. Add a handful of ice, seal, and shake hard for about 10 seconds. Strain into a cup, or just dump the whole cocktail into a cup with the ice as well.

THE NEW OLD-FASHIONED

This drink started as a joking way to make an "artisanal Fireball," but actually it's really good. Oops.

Ingredients

2 ounces (60 ml) good bourbon whiskey

1 ½ teaspoons spicy cinnamon syrup (see below)

1 teaspoon water

Twist of orange, if possible

Make It

In a cup combine the whiskey, syrup, and water and stir. Add a bit of ice and stir for another few seconds. Garnish with a twist of orange peel, if you have it.

SPICY CINNAMON SYRUP

Ingredients

1 cup (237 ml) water

1 cup (200 g) sugar

2 cinnamon sticks

1 teaspoon red pepper flakes

1 teaspoon angostura bitters

Make It

1. Combine water and sugar in a saucepan. Add cinnamon sticks and red pepper flakes. Bring to a boil, then turn down to a simmer and cook for 10 minutes.

2. Strain through a fine-mesh strainer and add angostura bitters. Stir to combine. Allow to cool, then transfer to a sealed container to store. Syrup will keep for about 3 weeks if kept cool or refrigerated.

Resources

If you have a local outfitter or camping gear store, I highly recommend that you purchase your gear through them. You'll be able to talk to knowledgeable, passionate people while also supporting local businesses with your dollars. But, for some additional guidance, here are a few online sources for some of our preferred gear and tips.

WWW.BACKCOUNTRY.COM
Back Country is a large outdoor company that carries camping gear and clothing from all of the major brands, so it's a great one-stop shop.

WWW.GSIOUTDOORS.COM
A whole company that specializes in outdoor cookware? Yes, please! And that's just what GSI Outdoors is. This is often my go-to source for camping cook pots and Dutch ovens or if I need specialized tools for upping the gourmet game in camp.

WWW.REI.COM
Like Back Country, REI (Recreational Equipment, Inc.) is a large outdoor retailer where you can find virtually anything you need. Plus you can become a member and earn rewards!

WWW.FROSTRIVER.COM
This a local outfitter here in Duluth, Minnesota, that focuses on canoe gear and hand-sewn packs.

WWW.ULTIMATECAMPGROUNDS.COM
Online home of the Ultimate Public Campgrounds Project, this site provides incredibly comprehensive information to help you find public campgrounds wherever your adventures may be taking you.

Acknowledgments

It took a village to teach me to camp, and that village sure stepped up with enthusiasm and bucketloads of fun and can-do attitude to support me in the creation of this book. Thank you, thank you to my whole community. I truly love you all so much and feel blessed to know you and learn from you. To name just a few names—Anna, Peter, Kelsey, Haakon, Marit, thank you for letting me talk your ears off and probe your minds for memories about your favorite family camping foods. To our beloved campfire crew—Sarah, Cal, Gigi, Annie, Janaki, Truman, Ellis—thank you times a million for all the time spent around bonfires eating more hot dogs and marshmallows than would seem humanly possible while waiting for other things to cook in cast-iron skillets. To everyone who joined in the photo fun—Jake, Hillary, Ansel, Matti, Marit, Haakon—thanks for lending your smiles, hands, and adorable children. Sorry we hopped them up on so much sugar. You knew this was coming—Mark and Sherry, thank you so much for all the support, the Dutch oven lessons, and for generously sharing your amazing stories. And Sherry, oh my gosh, your gift for finding treasures and curating props is unparalleled!!!! Thank you for letting us raid all of your gorgeous enamelware and pots and pans and linens. Hanna and Kady, thank you for your brilliance, talent, creativity, and your eyes for aesthetics. You sure know how to make a lot of brown food look good. I am so impressed, not only by your skill but by your amazing stamina. Thank you Thom, Marissa, Kari, and everyone at Quarto for your guidance, organizing (a skill I definitely always need a little assist with!), and also for bearing with me while trying to write through the ups and downs of a year in a pandemic.

To Kaitlin, thank you for being a rock, a rock star, and a lifelong bestie. Meeting you at age four is one of the biggest blessings in my life. Thanks for always being there for me. And thanks for all your amazing contributions to this book. Thank you for the advice, the expertise, the brainstorms, the reality checks, the giggles, and for all your bonkers amounts of help during the photo shoot days. None of this would have happened without you.

And most of all to my family. I mean, you can't write a family cookbook without a family now, can you? But mostly, I love you to the ends of the earth and beyond. Thank you Mom and Dad for being my role models and for raising me to be a woman of the woods and a lover of food. It's a good combination. Also, thank you for never leaving me at a way station in Nebraska. Thank you Aunty Kathy, Erik, Maria, Even, Eline, and little Emil for being my cheerleaders. And to Joel, Espen, and Vidar, thank you all for being you, you silly goons. You're my favorites. I love you all more than anything. Also, thank you for eating four dinners per day while this book was sorting itself out. I can tell you already miss it.

About the Author

EMILY VIKRE, PhD, is the co-founder and CEO of Vikre Distillery, an award-winning craft distillery in Duluth, Minnesota. A nationally recognized food and drinks writer, Emily has been a regular columnist for FOOD52 and has written for *Lucky Peach*, Minnesota Public Radio, and *Norwegian American Weekly*. She is the author of *Camp Cocktails: Easy, Fun, and Delicious Drinks for the Great Outdoors*, published by Quarto Publishing Group. She holds a PhD in food policy and behavioral theory from Tufts University. She is also a member of the board of Friends of the Boundary Waters Wilderness. When she isn't at work, you'll find her forest bathing, foraging, swimming, or cross-country skiing along the North Shore of Lake Superior with her husband, two young sons, and adorable mutt named Squid.

Index